THE FASTING COOKBOOK

ANGELA DOWDEN
NUTRITIONIST OF THE YEAR

100 **DELICIOUS RECIPES** FOR **100, 200,** AND **300 CALORIE MEALS**

hamlyn

Angela Dowden is a registered nutritionist who writes on diet and health for numerous newspapers and magazines. She was awarded the Nutrition and Health Writer/Broadcaster of the Year award in 2012.

An Hachette UK Company
www.hachette.co.uk
First published in Great Britain in 2013 by
Hamlyn a division of Octopus Publishing Group Ltd
Endeavour House, 189 Shaftesbury Avenue
London, WC2H 8JY
www.octopusbooks.co.uk

Distributed in the US by
Hachette Book Group USA
237 Park Avenue
New York NY 10017 USA

Distributed in Canada by
Canadian Manda Group
664 Annette Street
Toronto, Ontario, Canada M6S 2C8

ISBN 978-0-600-62984-9

A CIP catalogue record for this book is available from the British Library

Printed and bound in China

1 3 5 7 9 10 8 6 4 2

Standard kitchen level spoon and cup measurements are used in all recipes.

Ovens should be preheated to the specified temperature. If using a convection oven, follow the manufacturer's instructions for adjusting the time and temperature. Broilers should also be preheated.

This book includes dishes made with nuts and nut derivatives. It is advisable for those with known allergic reactions to nuts and nut derivatives and those who may be potentially vulnerable to these allergies, such as pregnant and nursing mothers, people with weakened immune systems, the elderly, babies, and children, to avoid dishes made with nuts and nut oils.

Contents

Introduction

If you've picked up this book, you may already be a convert to intermittent fasting. Alternatively, you may have heard about its benefits and are wondering whether to try it yourself. At the other end of the scale, you may be a battle-weary diet skeptic, still holding out a small hope you'll one day find the way to shape up and feel healthier permanently. Whatever your starting point or motivation, if you have a small or large amount of weight to lose, and would like to feel more comfortable in your own skin, it's for you, too.

So what is the fasting—or 5:2—approach to weight loss and how does it work? There are any number of ways people practice intermittent fasting, from one day of light eating a week to no food at all for several days in a row. The 5:2 approach—5 days of normal eating and 2 days on restricted calories—works well for most people because it's a pragmatic solution that steers a safe, doable, and yet effective path through these extremes.

How to use the book

The 5:2 plan allows normal eating (including treats and meals out) for five days a week and then restricts calorie intake to 500 calories a day for women and 600 calories for men (a quarter of the normal recommended daily intake) for the other two. For most people, it's the perfect compromise that allows for socializing, family life, and work commitments, while still introducing enough calorie control to make sure you lose weight at a healthy rate.

With its delicious and innovative recipe selection, this book shows just how flexibly you can consume your 500 or 600 calories to keep the hunger wolf from the door and, yes, even tickle your taste buds at the same time! It also includes some sweet treats that are suitable for a fast day.

Ultimately, you'll be losing weight by eating, overall, fewer calories than your body uses up. But where the 5:2 diet is particularly great is how wonderfully achievable it can make this task for food lovers. People who find success with 5:2 often report that they failed to lose weight in the past because cutting back every day was such a struggle—doing so for just a couple of days a week, albeit more drastically, is a much more attractive proposition. Better still, far from being a short-term fad, those who practice intermittent fasting find it is a lifestyle choice that they can stick to because it doesn't take over their whole life, doesn't demonize specific foods, and can even run alongside other supportive weight-loss grograms, such as online food diary methods.

As to the health benefits? As you lose body fat and get thinner, you can expect to greatly reduce your chance of having a heart attack or developing heart disease. And, in strands of research unrelated to the weight-loss benefits, there's a growing amount of science that shows that periodically putting your body into a fasted state may cause various chemical changes linked with lower risk of age-related diseases and higher chance of living healthier for longer.

Whether you're a 5:2 fan in search of food inspiration, or just intrigued to know more, you'll find something in this book for you. Read, digest, get thinner, and enjoy!

IS THE FASTING DIET FOR EVERYONE?

Most overweight adults can benefit from a 5:2 diet, but it should never be embarked on by children or adolescents, for whom any form of nutritional stress is undesirable. Also, do not do the 5:2 diet if any of the following apply (check with your medical health-care provider if you are uncertain).

- You are pregnant, trying to get pregnant, or breast-feeding.
- You are already at the bottom end of your healthy weight. You can check this using an online Body Mass Index (BMI) calculator—a BMI of 20 or less would indicate you are not a candidate for 5:2, or indeed any weight-loss program.
- You are an elite athlete or in training for a marathon or other big stamina event.
- You are diabetic.
- You have irritable bowel syndrome.
- You have been diagnosed with an eating disorder, either recently or in the past.

What is intermittent fasting?

People have fasted—out of choice or through necessity—for millennia, so the general concept is far from new. Interest was roused in the 1930s (and repeatedly since) when scientists found that restricting the calories fed to various animals and insects increased their life-span. The idea of severely restricting calories every other day—instead of by a smaller amount every day—came later, in 2003, with laboratory research carried out at the National Institute on Aging (NIA) in the United States. The concept of intermittent fasting—and more specifically the 5:2 diet—for managing weight reached a mass audience when Dr. Michael Mosley presented the theories in a BBC *Horizon* program aired on British television in August 2012.

Fasting is nothing new!

Fasting for physical well-being and spiritual reflection is as old as the hills and all of the big religions, such as Judaism, Buddhism, Christianity, and Islam, embrace it. It's only in modern times that we've become obsessed by the notion that we'll grow weak and depleted if we don't graze on food around the clock. In fact, you don't have to think too long about it to realize that a menu of regularly spaced meals and snacks is probably more alien to our body than periods of feast followed by periods of famine. For cavemen and women, there would undoubtedly have been periods when they were subsisting only on berries, roots, and leaves until the next animal kill, when they were able to stock up on concentrated calories ready for more lean times ahead.

Nowadays, despite being bombarded with never-ending eating opportunities, our bodies are still designed with biology and hormones that expect food to be scarce at some times and more plentiful at others. This is why many scientists believe intermittent fasting could be a particularly healthy and physiologically appropriate way to keep trim and fight aging.

As well as suiting our biology, intermittent fasting also works well on a psychological level. The "carrot" of being able to eat without depriving yourself for five days a week far outweighs the "stick" of two much tougher days each week.

Addressing fasting diet concerns

Any "new" diet or weight-loss program will probably attract critical attention, and intermittent fasting is no exception. This is especially the case given that there are any number of ways (of varying levels of sensibleness and safety) that you can do the diet, and any types of food you can include or avoid.

Suffice to say, as a registered nutritionist, I had to be completely confident that the particular version of 5:2 fasting described in these pages can do no harm. And, for the record, I am completely confident that this is so. However, to deal with some specific points that might worry you, read on.

HAVEN'T STUDIES SHOWN THAT PEOPLE FIND INTERMITTENT FASTING HARDER THAN NORMAL CALORIE COUNTING?
This worried me, too, when I read a 2011 paper by Dr. Michelle Harvie and the team at Genesis Breast Cancer Prevention, a charity in Manchester, England. It compared obese women following a 5:2-style program with obese women on modest calorie restriction

every day, and found fewer of those in the intermittent fasting group reported that they would continue with the program. Dr. Harvie has since modified and improved the diet, however, and in a further, more recent clinical trial, her subjects were significantly more likely to stick to the fasting program than normal calorie restriction. I guess this usefully illustrates the importance of finding a version of 5:2 eating that you can actually *enjoy*. Let's not pretend, however, that any one program will always work for everyone—if something doesn't work for you, don't do it!

FASTING MAY BE OKAY FOR MEN, BUT ISN'T IT BAD FOR WOMEN?

The basis of this argument seems to be that women have lower lean tissue levels and as such have less reserve if skipped meals lead to the breakdown of essential muscle. Even if this were a concern—and studies of moderate intermittent fasting programs suggest it's not—this is covered by eating modest amounts of protein on your fast day (see Fast Day Eating guidelines on page 19). Another small study that compared the experiences of eight nonobese men and women might also seem a blow to females, because it concluded that intermittent fasting seemed to "adversely affect glucose tolerance in nonobese women but not in nonobese men." However, the subjects were on a harsh program with no food at all for 36 hours in every 48-hour period. Obese women following much gentler routines, such as the one advocated in this book, show very good responses in blood glucose levels and markers of diabetes risk (see page 12).

I HEARD IT COULD AFFECT FERTILITY?

As long as you eat your 500 calories on fast days, you're not being too extreme and there is no evidence whatsoever that female fertility will be affected. Being very overweight is much more likely to affect your fertility, and 5:2 is an effective way to tackle being overweight. However, to be on the safe side, don't follow a 5:2 diet if you are actively trying for a baby. Being very thin will also affect fertility.

DOESN'T "FASTING" ENCOURAGE EATING DISORDERS?

We're very clear that you shouldn't try intermittent fasting if you have ever had an eating disorder. This is just to be safe in case it unearths any old obsessive behaviors. More lengthy forms of fasting may be somewhat addictive, but 5:2 isn't a food-free fast at all, it's just a restricted-calorie one. There is no evidence at all that it can trigger a new eating disorder.

HOW ABOUT BREAKFAST?

Skipping this meal is particularly frowned upon by experts, but most intermittent fasters will eat it on a fast day. However, don't force yourself to do so if you prefer not to; although breakfast eating is clearly associated with better health and weight, breakfast eaters also tend to have many other healthy habits, such as watching saturated fat intake and doing more exercise, which collectively explain the benefits.

ISN'T SKIPPING MEALS BAD FOR YOU?

If skipping meals is part of a generally erratic and unhealthy pattern of eating, where you lurch from one unhealthy snack to another in lieu of proper balanced meals, then yes. However, with the type of controlled food restriction advocated by 5:2, the focus is on getting good nutrition despite having very few calories. There's now also a lot of evidence showing that, far from being bad for you, periods with no or very little food intake are actually healthy, provided, as outlined on page 5 and above, you don't have a medical or psychological condition that prohibits it.

ARE FASTING PROGRAMS STRICT ENOUGH TO GET MAXIMAL HEALTH BENEFITS?

One criticism, usually from academic quarters, is that 5:2 fasting doesn't actually deliver as many health benefits as it could and that periods of 18–36 hours without food are needed for potential protection against conditions such as Alzheimer's and cancer. This is at odds with what's conventionally thought safe and sensible, so is there a sensible compromise? If you want to potentially maximize the benefits of 5:2, one way *may* be to try eating just one meal on your fast day, and to make it lunch or dinner (you could try two or three courses adding up to 500 or 600 calories from our recipe section). However, fasting in any prolonged fashion is beyond the remit of this book, and the focus of our 5:2 advice is safe and efficient weight loss, so never do anything that feels uncomfortable.

The health benefits

As with any emerging new science, intermittent fasting attracts a variety of expert opinion and debate, from "evidence that intermittent fasting can have health benefits is very strong" (Professor Mark Mattson, Chief of the Laboratory of Neurosciences at the U.S. National Institute on Aging) to "limited evidence base for intermittent fasting in general" (from the National Institutes of Health, or NIH, in Great Britain).

What's undeniable is that the research into the health benefits of intermittent fasting is really picking up and, although to date the number of human studies may have been somewhat small, this is rapidly changing, with new results coming out all the time.

In fact, so much so that it's hard to keep up unless you're immersed on a daily basis in this academic area—which is probably why www.nhs.uk scattered its review of 5:2 dieting with caveats warning readers it was an "unsystematic review" and "not an exhaustive 'last word' on the topic." Suffice to say, the top researchers in the area of intermittent fasting—most of them at American universities—tend to get a lot more excited and evangelical than serious academics normally have a wont to do when it comes to their particular areas of research. Many practice intermittent fasting themselves—and often hardcore versions—because they are so convinced of the benefits.

So what do we know are the benefits of intermittent fasting so far?

Weight loss

When you only eat 500 or 600 calories for two days a week and don't significantly overcompensate during the remaining five days (as evidence shows most people don't), it stands to reason that weight will start to drop. But research suggests that intermittent fasting may help people remove excess weight in a more efficient and effective way than normal calorie restriction.

In particular, a 2011 review by researchers at the University of Illinois at Chicago found that people who did alternate day fasting (a repeating pattern of one day unrestricted eating followed by one day of no- or low-calorie fasting) were more likely to retain higher amounts of muscle tissue while losing at least as much fat. This is important because muscle helps to keep your metabolic rate higher, in essence because it is much more metabolically active than other tissues. In short, by having a more muscular frame, you can continue to burn more calories all day every day, even when you are sitting down or sleeping, which is very helpful in managing your weight over the longer term.

What doesn't kill you makes you stronger

Research published in the *Journal of Nutritional Biochemistry* showed that feeding rats and mice only every other day improved the health and function of their brains, hearts, and other organs. Other studies have shown that mice and rats on intermittent fasts develop fewer cancers, are less prone to neurological disorders, and live 30 percent longer than their siblings that were fed every day. All this is fascinating information that's driving the new wave of human studies, but what's particularly interesting is that experts think it's the *stress* that fasting puts on the body that does the good!

According to Professor Mark Mattson—reported by *New Scientist* magazine to be the world's most cited neuroscientist—fasting is a type of hormesis, a process whereby organisms exposed to low levels of stress or toxins become more resistant to tougher challenges. For example, the mild biological stress induced by fasting causes cells in the heart and digestive tract to produce proteins that decrease heart rate and blood pressure and increase digestive motility (the movement of food through the digestive), reducing the risk of heart disease, stroke, and colon cancer. It seems to be a case of what doesn't kill you (i.e., managing on minimum food for a couple of days a week) makes you stronger!

Diabetes and blood sugar control

Any amount of weight loss in obese individuals, however it is achieved, will generally result in the body becoming more sensitive to insulin, which is an important step toward reducing the risk of diabetes (exercise has the effect of making you more responsive to insulin, too). But intermittent fasting could have a particularly good effect on your blood sugar control and diabetes risk.

In one of Dr. Michelle Harvie's studies for Genesis Breast Cancer Prevention at Manchester's Wyntheshawe Hospital, women who were on a 5:2-style intermittent fasting diet (largely milk and vegetables, adding up to 650 calories for two days each week, and a Mediterranean-style diet for the rest of the time), were compared with women who were restricted to 1,500 calories every day. In both groups, women lost weight, reduced their cholesterol levels, recorded lower blood pressures, and had reduced markers of breast cancer risk. When it came to reductions in fasting insulin and insulin resistance—both signs that diabetes risk has decreased—the benefits, although modest, were greater in the 5:2 diet group than those using conventional calorie restriction.

Heart disease

As I have alluded to, a reduction in cardiovascular risk factors—for example, LDL cholesterol (that's the "bad" type that carries cholesterol toward arteries, where it collects and causes "furring") and high blood pressure—can be expected on the 5:2 diet. Triglycerides in the blood will also tend to fall as you lose weight (put simply, this means that your blood is less sticky and, therefore, less liable to clot).

Much of the work in this area has been done by Dr. Krista Varady and her team at the University of Illinois at Chicago, with one of her scientific papers on the subject being entitled "Intermittent fasting combined with calorie restriction is effective for weight loss and cardio-protection in obese women" (November 2012). The research outlines how intermittent fasting, and wider, healthy weight loss, can benefit heart health. The title pretty much says it all!

Brain function

Much of the research into intermittent fasting actually started, and continues, in the healthy aging field, and brain aging in particular. At the U.S. National Institute on Aging, they've been investigating rats and mice that have been genetically engineered to develop Alzheimer's disease. Given normal circumstances, these animals show obvious signs of dementia by the time they are a year old (getting disorientated in a maze that they have previously been able to navigate with ease, for example), but when they're put on an on/off fasting program, they don't develop dementia until they're around 20 months, or much nearer the natural end of their lives.

What could be the reason? One thing that's been reported is that the fasting mouse brain produces more of a protein called BDNF (brain-derived neurotrophic factor), which stimulates the growth of new nerve cells in the hippocampus part of the brain, essential for learning and memory. There's certainly an evolutionary logic for the fasting state to be linked with better cognitive function, too; if you were hungry in caveman days, you needed your wits about you to track down the next meal and survive!

As yet, there are still many unknowns (for example, whether longer periods of fasting are needed than normally experienced on a 5:2 diet) and the human studies have still to be done, so it's impossible to say if intermittent fasting will help to prevent dementia. But it's certainly a very interesting area of research, and one to watch.

Cancer

Much of the published research into the potential disease-protective effects of intermittent fasting involve measuring a biological marker named insulin-like growth factor-1 (IGF-1), which is known to be associated with cancer. Fasting has the effect of reducing IGF-1 levels, at least temporarily, and also seems to stimulate genes that repair our cells.

How a reduction in IGF-1 translates into successful real-world outcomes (i.e., a reduced chance of people getting cancer) is still unclear, however. One 2007 clinical review did look at "real-world" health outcomes and concluded that intermittent fasting (specifically, alternate day fasting, which usually has minimum 18-hour periods without food) may have a protective effect against cancer, as well as heart disease and diabetes. However, it concluded "research is required to establish definitively the consequences," which is a fair reflection of the science as it currently is. In short, how effective intermittent fasting is against cancer relative to other healthy-eating or weight-loss programs is still to be clarified.

COULD FASTING MAKE YOU HAPPIER?

Anecdotally, many 5:2 eaters say their low-calorie intake makes them feel more clear-headed, more able to concentrate, and even more cheerful. It's uncertain as to why this should be, but feeling more upbeat will certainly make it easier to refuse that slice of cake!

Getting started

The beauty of the 5:2 diet is that, beyond the requirement for two 500- or 600-calorie days a week, there are no firm rules and it's very flexible. As with all new healthy habits, however, it can take time to adjust and the hunger aspect can initially be hard. On the plus side, the results you begin to see and feel within a short time mean your fast days will quickly become less of a chore, and even something you can begin to enjoy. Preparation and planning are key.

Choose your fasting days

As a first step, you'll need to decide which days will work best for you as fasting days. This may evolve over time, or from week to week, according to your circumstances. As a general rule, you're more probable to stay with the program if you can repeat the same two days every week, so try to choose days that you'll need to deviate from only infrequently. For example, don't pick a Tuesday if this is the day when a friend will probably invite you around for lunch, or a Friday if you're going to be tempted by a takeout after work. For obvious reasons, weekend days may not be such good fasting days either, but everyone's different and you should choose what works for you.

Whether you run the two days consecutively or apart is also up to you, and there isn't enough research to say definitively that one way or another is best. Many people doing 5:2 for themselves, and not in the context of a highly monitored clinical trial, find it easiest in terms of managing hunger and keeping on track to have a gap between fasting days. Having this breather between days helps you feel your dieting task is neither too hard nor too long. However, it may be that you're more probable to get the two days done if you run them back to back. If doing two days together suits you better, and you feel energetic and motivated, there's no reason why you shouldn't do it this way (and it may even be better for your body).

THE GENDER DIVIDE

On a fasting day:

- If you're a man, you should have no more than 600 calories.
- If you're a woman, you should have no more than 500 calories.
- It is a fact that, even if a man and a woman weigh the same, the man will usually burn more calories than the woman because he has a higher proportion of muscle (see page 8).

Fast day meals

The second decision to make is how you will spread your 500 or 600 calories over the fasting day. Again, this is decided on personal preference, usually honed through trial and error. A satisfying format for many people is to bookend their day with two meals— a 100–200-calorie breakfast and a 300-calorie dinner, for example, with the possibility of 100 calories or so for snacking or another small meal in between if desired. Other people report they are happier if they don't eat their first morsel until brunch or lunch, while still others (usually men, on anecdotal evidence) prefer saving up their calories for just one reasonable-size meal—either a lunch or an evening meal.

One argument for leaving your first calorie intake until lunch or later is that the stretch of time you go without food is longer—perhaps 18 hours or more—which some researchers have surmised may be associated with potentially bigger health benefits (see page 9). (By comparison, the longest you'd go without food if you eat breakfast on your fasting day will probably be around 12 hours.)

However, many people, perhaps women in particular, prefer to graze their way through fast days, and Dr. Michelle Harvie's research offers some reassurance here. It found that obese women eating three small, evenly spaced mini meals on two nonconsecutive fasting days per week lost weight efficiently and also reduced inflammatory chemicals that increase breast cancer risk.

The main point is to find what suits you and not to force yourself into a routine that doesn't fit your lifestyle. We simply don't know the optimum food-free stretch, if there is any optimum at all.

Keep a food diary

To find a pattern of food intake that enables you to stick to your 5:2 plans and achieve sustainable weight loss, try keeping a food and mood diary. Making a note of how you feel physically and mentally on fast days can be an effective way to track how well you're coping with the program. Simply write down what foods/meals you eat, when you have them, and any accompanying feelings of hunger, mood, or wavering willpower. Registering when you feel at your weakest and strongest on a fast day can help you to tailor future fast days so that they are easier.

What does 500 calories look like?

Admittedly not a lot—but then that is, after all, somewhat the point! As a rough guide, 500 calories would be:

- Breakfast: A small bowl (¾ cup/1 ounce) of bran flakes with ½ cup low-fat milk, plus a handful (½ cup/3 ounces) each of blueberries and strawberries (200 calories).
- Dinner: About 1⅔ cup (6½ ounces) canned bean soup followed by 3½ ounces shrimp with a dessert bowl of salad of arugula, bell peppers, tomato, and cucumber dressed with 1 tablespoon of low-fat balsamic dressing (250 calories).
- Snack: ½ banana (50 calories).
- Men have another 100 calories to play with, which is the equivalent of adding half a slice of toast spread with 2 teaspoons of peanut butter.

If this looks daunting, don't worry—there are plenty of tips for making your fasting day as painless as possible in the following pages. While most intermittent fasters will find it challenging at first, the process gets much easier as your body adapts.

More than 500 or 600 calories?

Some programs allow up to 700 calories on fast days, but if you increase calories on these two days you'll probably have to look at introducing some restrictions on the other five days, too. The amount of 500 or 600 calories is 25 percent of the normal average calorie requirement, and emulates the protocol used by some preliminary but successful alternate day fasting human studies completed at the University of Illinois at Chicago (a 5:2 fasting program is a more achievable version of alternate day fasting, and you'll probably find it easier to follow).

While a handful of calories either way isn't going to make much difference, if it becomes obvious you're going to breach 500 or 600 calories by a large amount, abandon ship and count the day as a nonfast one.

TOP TIPS FOR BEGINNERS

- The day before your first fast, eat well and aim to go to bed feeling neither hungry nor overfull. Getting an early night is good preparation. Trying to stuff in as much food as late as possible so you don't feel hungry tomorrow is not!
- Do your eating homework so that you know how you are going to spend your 500 or 600 calories, and which meals you are going to spread them between. Use the recipes in this book as inspiration and make sure you are stocked up with the requisite ingredients.
- Try to make your environment as devoid of food temptations as possible, which means making sure a stray slice of apple pie isn't the thing screaming, "eat me!" when you open the refrigerator.
- Arm yourself with some kind of calorie counter—there is one to get you started on pages 140–142—or you can use an online app or Web site.
- Be aware that choosing a less busy day to start your fasting may not be the best approach. As long as you have your food choices preplanned, a day with plenty to keep you occupied may be better.
- If you find your first fast too hard and have to give in, you've probably just chosen the wrong day. Don't give up and try again another time, but leave it for a few days.

Fast day eating

Theoretically, you could have a large burger and endless cups of black coffee on a fast day and be within your calorie allowance, but clearly this wouldn't be good for you! Instead, it's a great idea to use your fasting day to make balanced and healthy choices, using the following guidelines.

Eat five a day

Your fast day is the perfect opportunity to fill up on fruit and vegetables because these foods are bulky and low in calories, take up plenty of room on your plate (a psychological boost), and are linked with a lower risk of killer diseases, such as heart disease and cancer. Green leafy vegetables, such as spinach, kale, watercress, arugula, broccoli, and cabbage, are particularly low in calories, as are berries, such as strawberries and raspberries, which you'll often find in convenient form in the freezer section of the supermarket. Tomatoes, bell peppers, orange-fleshed melons, and butternut squash join the low-calorie corner—the wonderful thing about all these colorful fruit and vegetables is they consistently appear in superfood lists because of their high antioxidant content (antioxidants are the component in fruit and vegetables that mop up the free radicals that can damage our cells).

In short, by using your fast day as a chance to eat at least five colouful portions of fruit and vegetables a day (a portion is around 3 ounces, or roughly a handful), you'll be boosting your health as well as benefiting your waistline.

Dairy and beans

These two deserve a special mention because they're unusual in providing a combination of carbs and protein in one easy package and are a great source of vitamins and minerals. They can be easy on the waistline, too—fat-free Greek yogurt (a great topping for fruit) has only 57 calories in a scant ½-cup (3½-ounce) serving, while canned lima beans (fabulous to bulk out a salad) have 56 calories in a ⅓-cup (2½-ounce) serving.

Include lean protein

The lowest calorie lean protein sources (all weighing in at less than 100 calories for a 3½-ounce serving) include shrimp, tofu, and tuna canned in water, although broiled fish, eggs, and chicken breast are also good choices. Including one or more of these protein foods on a fast day is recommended, because you will more probably preserve valuable muscle tissue during periods of calorie restriction when protein is consumed (exercising helps conserve muscle tissue, too). Another big bonus is that protein is particularly good at keeping you full, so can help to keep hunger pangs at bay for longer. Digesting it also uses up more calories than does digesting other nutrients, which is all a bonus when it comes to your diminishing middle!

Choose quality carbs

Admittedly, you won't be able to eat very big carb portions on a fast day (there are around 100 calories in just one slice of bread, for example), but it's a good idea to make sure any modest portions you do choose are as unprocessed or nutrient rich as possible, and to focus on higher fiber choices where you can. Wheat breads, rolled oats, whole-wheat pasta, pearl barley, fortified whole-grain breakfast cereals, and potatoes in their skins tend to have a relatively low glycemic index or GI, which means they raise blood sugar levels only relatively slowly, helping to keep blood sugar, energy, and appetite levels more controlled.

Although sticking to the correct quantity of calories is the key priority on fast day, the quality of those calories is important, too, so try not to get sidetracked by too many sweet foods. We've included a few sweet treats you can get away with and enjoy in the recipe section, but too many high GI, sugary carbs can really challenge your ability to stay on track, because they can cause your blood sugar levels to fluctuate, heightening feelings of hunger.

Beverage options

It is important to stay well hydrated on fast days (see page 28), but with the exception of low-fat milk (or a milk alternative, such as soy milk), many drinks can be a wasteful, nonfilling way to spend calories. Your best options on a fast day are calorie-free drinks, such as

PERFECT FAST DAY PROPORTIONS

- Concentrate on fruit and vegetables (steamed, broiled, stir-fried, or in soups and salads) as your main stomach-filling priority (up to 200 calories).
- Most of the remaining calories (300 or 400) will be best spent on low GI carbohydrate-rich and/or protein-rich foods.
- Use any leftover calories you have as you want (see the lists of up to 50-calorie and up to 100-calorie snack suggestions on pages 36–37). However, choosing more nutritious foods is always best.

black coffee and tea (but try not to drink more caffeine than you would normally), herbal teas, diet drinks, and, of course (and best of all), good old water. To jazz it up, try a sparkling variety and add a squeeze of lime or lemon.

Alcohol is one of the least sensible choices of all (even the smallest glass of wine has around 100 calories and could stimulate your appetite), so use your fast days to abstain from alcohol altogether and give your liver two days a week of much needed rest.

Fast day feel-full tips

- Water is the perfect slimline filler, either drunk on its own to temporarily take the edge off a hunger pang or, more particularly, incorporated within food to increase satiety (the feeling of fullness that food imparts). Chunky soups plus a lot of fruit and vegetables can work particularly well on a fast day because they'll help to make your stomach feel full.
- Airy foods take up more space on your plate (so, psychologically, it feels like you're being presented with more food), as well as in your stomach. One study by Professor Barbara Rolls at Pennsylvania State University, published in the journal *Appetite*, compared the same snack in a puffed and nonpuffed version and found that those receiving the airy snack ate 73 percent more in volume, but consumed 21 percent fewer calories. Rice cakes are the ultimate airy food, and a whipped mousse (which can have fewer than 80 calories per container) is ok for a quick dessert if you can't do without.
- Protein-rich foods are particularly good at inducing satiety. One theory is that they stimulate the release of hunger-controlling hormones in the digestive tract. The protein in eggs seems particularly good at keeping you full, so try them.
- Whole-grain versions of breakfast cereals, breads, pasta, rice, and noodles take longer to chew and are more satisfying, because the fiber they contain provides bulk but no calories. Fiber also has a slowing effect on the passage of food through the digestive tract, which has the effect of keeping you fuller for longer. The serving size of bread or pasta you can have on a fast day is small, but choosing a "wheat," not "white," version can help to make it more filling.
- Focus on foods made from scratch. On average, foods that aren't highly processed, already prepared and packaged, or high in sugar will tend to be lower GI and keep your blood sugar levels on a more even keel.

Don't estimate!

Building up an accurate picture of what actually constitutes 500 or 600 calories (see page 16) is one of the most educational and interesting aspects of the 5:2 diet. It can help you understand what constitutes a healthy portion and might also give a clue as to why you ended up needing to lose a few pounds in the first place.

It won't come as a surprise, then, that "estimates" and "educated guesses" are definitely not okay when it comes to calculating your fast day calories. With the best will in the world, you'll almost certainly be wrong, which will jeopardize your weight loss and dilute

WHAT ABOUT SWEETENERS?

Sugar substitutes, including aspartame, sucralose, and more recently stevia, have been approved by the U.S. government and health authorities the world over, yet there still seems to be a host of scare stories circulating on how they could actually make us fatter or even cause cancer. In the end, it's up to you if you want to use them or not, but if adding a little sweetness to a bowl of berries or to a cup of tea makes you more inclined to stay on track with your 5:2 diet, then go ahead and use them. Unless you're eating sweeteners in vast quantities, they probably won't do any harm and are a much better bet on fast day than spoonfuls of sugar.

the health benefits. If you're not convinced, try seeing if you can correctly estimate the "recommended" 1-ounce (¾-cup) serving of flake-style breakfast cereal, such as bran flakes. Most people pour nearer to 2–2½ ounces (1⅔–2 cups) into the bowl, which can add more than 100 "accidental" calories and completely destroy a fasting day. If you don't own a kitchen scale and measuring cups (for both dry and liquid ingredients), you need to lay your hands on both. Electronic kitchen scales are available at large department stores, and measuring cups don't require a great investment. Make sure you also have some standard kitchen measuring spoons in your kitchen drawer.

At first, you should weigh everything until you've got a clearer idea of what different-size servings weigh. Your idea of a medium apple—3½ ounces with peel but no core, according to official publications—may be different to mine or someone else's. It's also important to measure the ingredients carefully when you're making the recipes in this book, so they don't exceed the calorie counts given. If it seems like a pain, it's really not—it's actually fun learning about calories and serving sizes and, because you're only doing it two days a week and you're not eating that much on those days either, it's not an onerous task. Look at it as a chance to really understand what you are putting into your mouth.

"OFF" DAY EATING

Of necessity, some time has been spent explaining about fasting days, what to eat on them, and how to make sure they're successful. But let's not forget that the beauty of 5:2, and the core reason that it appeals to, and works for, so many people, is that you can have five days each week without worrying about cutting a single calorie.

Does that mean you can truly eat anything you wan, too? Well, yes, but naturally there are limits. The good news? Studies consistently show that contrary to what you might expect, intermittent fasters are actually very unlikely to go on a big binge on their "off" days. Instead of making your appetite more extreme, 5:2 dieting seems to help naturally regulate it so you enjoy only as much food as you need when you aren't fasting. That said, if your journey to 5:2 eating has involved a lifetime of flip-flopping between failed diets and bingeing, it may take longer for a healthy relationship with food to develop.

What to expect when fasting

If you have a BMI of 25 or more (use an online calculator to check your BMI), when you start your 5:2 eating plan you can expect to lose weight at an average rate of 1 pound a week until you stabilize at a healthy weight within the 18.5–25 BMI range. However, as with any form of calorie restriction, the amount you lose will vary from week to week, so expect highs, lows, and plateaus along the way. In the beginning, you may lose weight quickly 2–3 pounds isn't unusual in the first week—which can be particularly motivating. The flipside is that you risk becoming despondent in the weeks that follow if your weight loss fluctuates or slows down.

The key to success is always to have the bigger picture in mind—there may be disappointments along the way, but all the evidence suggests that in the longer term you will succeed. While the path may not be entirely smooth, no other dieting program can boast that you can eat without calorie restriction for five days a week and still be 14 pounds lighter in three to four months.

Measuring your progress

Before you begin the 5:2 diet, it's a good idea to know what your starting point is so you can measure your progress along the way. Some people say they prefer not to use a scale and are happy just to measure their progress in terms of a looser waistband, but this can often be about denial. No one is forcing you to weigh and measure, but if your weight has been creeping ever upward and you haven't been tracking it, it is probably best to bite the bullet, get on the scale, and face up to what your starting point may be.

MONITORING YOUR WEIGHT

Research findings from America's National Weight Control Registry—a database of people who have maintained a weight loss of 30 pounds or more for at least one year or more—show that 75 percent of weight watchers use regular weighing as part of their success strategy, and most diet and health professionals now believe that weekly monitoring of weight is a marker of diet success.

Newer bathrooms scales will also give you a read out of your percentage body fat, which should show a pleasing downward trend as the weeks go by. Do be aware, however, that different scales can give different body fat readings and even the same scales will register ups and downs from one day to the next, depending on factors such as time of day and how much fluid you've consumed. As with your weight, it's the trend over time that matters, so don't get hung up over individual measurements. Even small reductions in internal fat lower heart disease and diabetes risk.

WAIST MEASUREMENT

Another simple but effective way to measure your progress is with a tape measure around your middle. Measure at the place where your waist is naturally narrowest or, if this is hard to define, at the midpoint between the top of your hip bone and the bottom of your ribs. This measurement is a reasonable proxy for the amount of internal fat you have in the central region and in turn a good marker for heart disease, high blood pressure, and diabetes risk. As your waist measurement falls, your risk of developing any of these conditions is steadily reduced.

For men, those health risks move from high to medium as their waist measurement falls below 40 inches and to low risk when the measurement goes below 37 inches. For women, the respective figures are 34½ inches and 31½ inches. People of Asian backgrounds tend to have a higher proportion of body fat to muscle, so they need to achieve smaller waist measurements than those of Caucasians to achieve the same level of risk reduction.

As you progress with 5:2 fasting and the weight continues to drop off, you can also expect your level of LDL cholesterol (see page 12) to decrease, your blood pressure to come down, and your blood glucose level to shift downward. Other biomarkers—for example, those that predict cancer risk (see page 13)—will also probably improve.

Overstretched medical health-care providers tend not to be pleased when "worried well" patients demand repeated tests for no good medical reason. And less run-of-the-mill blood tests—for example, for IGF-1, which has been tracked in some intermittent fasting trials—may not be paid for by health insurance companies. However, your health-care provider may be happy to do simple but important checks on your blood pressure and cholesterol level, both now and after you've lost about 14 pounds or so. If not, some pharmacies offer a fully validated cholesterol check, which is relatively inexpensive.

Dealing with hunger

At first, those gripping hunger pangs can seem insistent on fast days. But the good news is that those feelings definitely become much less intense, with most long-term 5:2 devotees stating that they are no longer unduly troubled by fast day hunger after a few weeks. Another possibility is that intermittent fasters simply learn to embrace the feeling and not to be fazed by it.

Getting on top of initial hunger pangs can be as simple as actually experiencing those feelings and realizing that you can come out the other side without collapsing in a pile on the floor or dying of starvation. We're so programmed to eat at the slightest twinge of hunger that feeling anything more than slightly peckish can actually be alien and even a little scary. In time, when you realize nothing horrible is going to happen if you feel hungry for a day, this will change and you can actually learn to appreciate the physical sensations of hunger you get on a fast day, knowing that you are in tune with your body and have tackled the art of being able to savor food without overloading your system.

Exercise and fasting

An exercise program can definitely complement your 5:2 weight-loss progress, and will provide many attendant health benefits, such as stronger bones and a healthier heart. But how should you negotiate exercise on a fast day? The old wisdom was that you should be fueled well prior to exercise, but the latest evidence suggests that modest activity in the fasted state is actually good for you. In particular, exercising in the fasted state means that the body has to use fat as its primary fuel, which is good news for the disappearance of those love handles! Another benefit of exercising on an empty

stomach appears to be that you'll build muscle better when you do get around to eating in the postexercise period.

In a nutshell, there's no reason you shouldn't work out on your fast day, with the ideal being to exercise when you are feeling hungry, perhaps in the afternoon, and then to follow with one of your fast day meals. However, common sense must come into play, and if you're new to exercise, it's probably best to ease yourself into physical activity on only nonfast days. There's also some suggestion that women are better doing weights on fasting days (while men can particularly benefit from cardio work). Listening to your body is essential, and you should always stop exercising immediately if you feel faint, dizzy, or light-headed.

HOW ACTIVE SHOULD I BE?

Official guidelines suggest that for optimum health benefits you should be physically active (at the level of brisk walking or gentle cycling, for example) for at least 30 minutes five times a week. If you're doing something more vigorous, such as running or playing a racquet sport, you can get away with 75 minutes, or three 25-minute sessions a week. On top of this, one or two 20-minute sessions with weights are also recommended to maintain muscle tone and lean tissue levels, particularly in the over 40s.

10 ways to make the fasting diet work for you

1 Be flexible

The 5:2 program is definitely not a prescriptive diet with a big list of "dos" and "don'ts" that you may have been used to in the past. That's a plus point, but it can also be a little off-putting at first if you're used to being told exactly what you can and can't do as part of a weight-loss program.

The secret to finding the version for you is to be prepared to road test different fasting day routines until you find the one that works best. When it comes down to it, the chance to switch fasting days around is the key attraction of 5:2, and you should feel free to exploit that flexibility to it's fullest. One of the key deciding factors as to whether a diet works for you is how easily it fits around your existing lifestyle. This one of the key reasons why 5:2 attracts and retains followers.

2 Keep well hydrated

Fluid is your friend on fast days because it helps to give a sensation of stomach fullness, at least temporarily. Because it's also possible to confuse hunger with thirst, keeping up your intake of fluids at all times will prevent you falling foul of this potentially waist-widening mix-up. As a bonus, water is needed for every chemical reaction in the body, including burning fat.

However, don't think you must stick to plain water if you don't want to—black tea and coffee, herbal tea, and calorie-free beverages all count toward your fluid intake, too.

Most fresh fruit is more than 85 percent water and contains fiber, so it is good at keeping you both hydrated and full.

3 Find a fasting buddy

Research shows that when you're tackling your weight, you'll do better if you have someone doing it alongside you. For example, a study at the University of Pennsylvania found that 66 percent of the people dieting with friends had maintained their weight loss after 10 months compared to only 24 percent of those who were dieting on their own.

There's no particular reason that you'll need more support with 5:2 than any other program, and, in fact, many people do it successfully all by themselves because the periods of food deprivation are short and manageable. However, if a partner or friend wants to do it with you, you should jump at the chance for the extra support it brings.

4 Keep out of temptation's way

Fasting days are surprisingly doable, and with a positive mindset and some forward menu planning, you can even sit down for an evening meal (albeit with a different mix of foods on your plate) with the rest of the family. But—and it's a big and fairly logical but— there's simply no point putting yourself in temptation's way if you can avoid it.

Research at Cornell University's Food and Brand Lab in America has identified visibility and convenience as the two biggest drivers of mindless eating, with "out of sight" being a key strategy to successful calorie control. So taking steps as simple as keeping cookies in an opaque container or in a drawer, or moving a bowl of candies from your office desk to a filing cabinet a distance away can markedly increase your chances of staying on track on a fast day.

However, if you are faced with a food temptation, psychologists believe tightening muscles is so closely tied to determination that simply doing it can muster up greater willpower to resist. In studies, subjects were more probable to think they could resist chocolate cake while flexing their biceps, while others were better able to resist unhealthy foods at a snack bar while holding a pen woven through spread fingers (thus engaging their hand muscles). It's not hard to imagine how clenching helps, and balling your fists is certainly worth a try when faced with a strong temptation to break your fast.

5 Save chocolate for "off" days

Quite apart from the fact that you'll only be able to have a disappointingly teeny amount, one small study has suggested that eating chocolate when we are hungry may heighten our general desire for it. Conversely, eating it when we are full may "train" us out of a craving. Researchers at University College London split students into two groups, giving both groups half a bar of chocolate twice a day. After two weeks, the half that had been told to eat their chocolate rations on an empty stomach reported a stronger craving than before. By contrast, the students who had been eating the chocolate on a full stomach craved chocolate less and even reported that it now seemed somewhat less pleasant to the taste.

6 Consider online food shopping

Patrolling the aisles with your shopping cart can give you a small amount of exercise, but you may find that it's better to do shop online and go for a run instead! The reason? When you're shopping for fast-day food, supermarkets can be a toxic environment in the sense that the sights, smells, and deli counters can lure you to put things in your cart that you hadn't put on your list and didn't intend to buy. On your five "off" days, you can, of course, choose whatever foods you want, but many people do find they start to develop a natural inclination to eat a more balanced and healthy diet overall, which online shopping is potentially more supportive of. Certainly, if your grocery store starts to involve a lot of label reading (often in a challenging letter size), it may be easier to do this food sleuthing at the click of a mouse instead of in the supermarket itself.

7 Stay positive about weight loss

Virtually all people trying to lose weight will experience phases when they continue to stay at the same weight for what seems like a frustratingly long period of time. In actuality, it's probable to be only a few weeks, and anecdotally 5:2 eaters seem to experience fewer plateaus, possibly because of the constant switch between higher and lower calorie intakes and because levels of lean tissue (with a higher energy expenditure than fat) are maintained. However, if you do experience a plateau, a positive mindset is key. Try to focus on the weight you have lost and consider every week that you stick with your fast days as a success that's worth patting yourself on the back for. Traditional "diets" often aren't sustainable, but with 5:2 you should find it easier to keep on keeping on, such that you do succeed in the end. In reality, it's only plateaus that happen early on that tend to be a problem. Most established 5:2 fans are so wedded to their routine, weight loss becomes purely a bonus. On a practical level, increasing your activity level a little can help shake you out of a plateau. It's good to vary your routine, too, because your body will work harder at something it is not accustomed to.

8 Get more sleep

The evidence that insufficient sleep correlates to higher body weight has been piling up, and the latest strand of evidence suggests junk food may be particularly appealing to tired brains. When scientists at St. Luke's-Roosevelt Hospital Center and Columbia University in New York used high-tech brain scans to measure responses to unhealthy foods (such as pepperoni pizza and candies) versus healthier options (oatmeal and fruit), they found that the brain's reward center lit up more at the sight of junk food if the subjects tested were fatigued.

The take-home message? Get plenty of sleep, particularly the night before a fast day. At the very least, it's good for your general well-being; at best, it may also help keep up your resolve to stick with 5:2.

9 Keep busy

The devil may make work for idle hands, but you will also probably end up with your hands in the cookie jar if you're bored or not very busy. Part of planning a successful fasting day is, therefore, thinking about what you will do to occupy yourself as well as what you will eat. The most successful days are those when you have a particularly engrossing work project, are focusing on caring for children, or (hopefully this will happen from time to time), just enjoying a day out.

10 Don't be hard on yourself

If you have to miss a few fasting days because of vacations or other life events, don't get upset with yourself. There's always tomorrow or next week and you're meant to be living a life, not enduring a life sentence!

Intermittent fasting for life

Once you've reached the weight you're happy with, what next? As you've read through these pages, I hope you've become convinced that intermittent fasting, or 5:2, could well be something you incorporate into your life long term, as an active lifestyle choice. When bigger, longer studies into intermittent fasting emerge, as they undoubtedly will, the optimal way to continue intermittent fasting so that you can maximize any health benefits and keep your weight maintained will almost certainly become more apparent.

For now, the consensus approach from most people doing 5:2 who have already reached their ideal weight and don't want to become any slimmer is to switch to 500- or 600-calorie fasting just one day a week (a 6:1 diet). A small study showed people who had lost weight could keep it off by doing this, although another approach, if you want to keep a slightly firmer watch on your weight, would be to continue with two fast days—but let them creep up to, say, 700 calories.

Some people may find they can manage by using 5:2 fasting now and again (intermittent intermittent fasting, if you like), or to stop for longer periods or even altogether. These folk will be the ones who have become confident that they can now trust their own eating intuition to keep them safe from weight gain. In short, they can now trust their inbuilt hunger and fullness mechanisms (that were there all the time) to stay happily at their optimum weight.

Whatever your approach, remember that you should always obtain pleasure from your eating and your diet should never become a horrible chore. If you choose intermittent fasting as your ongoing method of optimizing health and weight, the recipes and suggested plans that follow should make that eminently possible for as long as you choose.

4-week fast day meal planner

Week 1

Day 1

Breakfast	1 poached egg on half a slice of whole-wheat toast spread with 1 teaspoon of low-fat spread and 1 medium (3-ounce) tomato, broiled	163 calories
Lunch or snack	1 rounded tablespoon of nonfat Greek yogurt with 1 cup (3½ ounces) cucumber and red bell pepper sticks	60 calories
Dinner	Asian Steamed Chicken Salad (see page 94)	273 calories
		496 calories

If you're a man: Add 2 tablespoons (½ ounce) of plain peanuts to the chicken salad

Day 2

Breakfast	1 Blueberry Bran Muffin (see page 45)	142 calories
Lunch or snack	1 apple and 1 satsuma	75 calories
Dinner	Red Snapper with Baked Tomatoes (see page 99)	287 calories
		504 calories

If you're a man: Add 1¼ cups (10 ounces) of store-bought fresh carrot and cilantro soup at lunch

Week 2

Day 1

Breakfast	¾-cup (1-ounce) serving of bran flakes with ½ cup low-fat milk and ½ cup (3 ounces) of blueberries	180 calories
Lunch or snack	2 clementines and 1 kiwi	73 calories
Dinner	Butternut Squash & Ricotta Frittata (see page 68)	248 calories
		501 calories

If you're a man: Serve yourself a bigger bowl of cereal (1½ cups/2 ounces bran flakes and ¾ cup low-fat milk) at breakfast

Day 2

Breakfast	½ plain bagel topped with 2 tablespoons (1 oz) light cream cheese and 2 ounces smoked salmon	270 calories
Lunch or snack	1 slice of cantaloupe and 1 clementine	45 calories
Dinner	Aromatic Steamed Mussels (see page 108)	185 calories
		500 calories

If you're a man: Top the melon with 2–3 slices of prosciutto

Week 3

Day 1

Breakfast	Oatmeal made with ½ cup (2 ounces) oats and 1 cup (7 fl oz) skim milk, plus ⅔ cup (3 ounces) raspberries. Add a sweetener, if desired	269 calories
Lunch or snack	1 large plum (about 3½ ounces, with the pit)	31 calories
Dinner	Fish & Tomato Curry (see page 105) with a handful of watercress leaves	199 calories
		499 calories

If you're a man: Add half a slice of toast spread with 2 teaspoons (⅓ ounce) of peanut butter

Day 2

Breakfast	1 medium apple	53 calories
Lunch or snack	Lime & Ginger Shrimp Coleslaw (see page 74)	143 calories
Dinner	Masala Roast Cod (see page 98) followed by baked rhubarb	300 calories
		496 calories

If you're a man: Have 2 plain poppadums with the cod

Week 4

Day 1

Breakfast	1 slice of whole-wheat toast spread with 1 teaspoon of low-fat spread and yeast extract, and ¾ cup (3½ ounces) of raspberries	147 calories
Lunch or snack	3½ ounces canned skinless, boneless sardines in tomato sauce on a bed of bagged salad greens, and 6 cherry tomatoes	183 calories
Dinner	Russian Meatballs (see page 113) with 7 cherry tomatoes	169 calories
		499 calories

If you're a man: Have the sardines on a slice of toast

Day 2

Breakfast	Fruity Summer Milkshake (see page 40)	89 calories
Lunch or snack	1 rounded tablespoon of nonfat Greek yogurt and 1 cup (3½ ounces) cucumber and red bell pepper sticks	60 calories
Dinner	Lemony Scallop Skewers (see page 107) followed by Strawberry Roulade (see page 138)	348 calories
		497 calories

If you're a man: Add a banana

PORTION PERFECTION

Tasty meals are your absolute ally on fast day, but if something tastes too good, you need to watch yourself carefully. Making sure you are scrupulous with portion sizes when you're serving the recipes is important. Choosing dishes that just serve one may be a best if you're dieting solo and can't be sure you have enough self-control.

Give yourself a treat

50 snacks up to 100 calories

- 1 medium apple (4 ounces): 53 calories
- about 9 (½ ounce) plain almonds (weigh them because they vary): 88 calories
- 1 warm crumpet or English muffin spread with yeast extract (no butter): 100 calories
- 2 cups (½ ounce) salted popcorn: 83 calories
- 3½ ounces store-bought lemon and cilantro shrimp: 80 calories
- 1 slice of prosciutto wrapped around a breadstick: 58 calories
- 1 rye crispbread with 2 tablespoons (1 ounce) light cream cheese: 82 calories
- 1 individually wrapped mini malt loaf (for lunch boxes): 95 calories
- 2 ounces reduced-fat shrimp cocktail: 83 calories
- 1½ tablespoon s(½ ounce) roasted, salted peanuts: 89 calories
- 1 rounded tablespoon (1 ounce) of tzatziki or nonfat Greek yogurt with 1 cup (3½ ounces) cucumber and red bell pepper sticks: 60 calories
- scant ½ cup (3½ ounces) fat-free strawberry yogurt: 79 calories
- 1 light cheese triangle and 1 slice of cucumber spread on 1 rice cake: 82 calories
- 1 medium banana: 95 calories
- ¾ cup (7 ounces) canned lentil soup: 95 calories
- 1 falafel with 1 teaspoon of sweet chili sauce: 65 calories
- ½ cup (3 ounces) cooked chicken breast pieces: 90 calories
- 1 cold vegetarian sausage: 86 calories
- 1 vegetarian chicken nugget with 2 teaspoons of sweet chili dipping sauce: 87 calories
- about 2 (½ ounce) Brazil nuts: 82 calories (weigh them because they vary)
- ¾ ounce wafer-thin ham, 1 tomato, and a little mustard: 81 calories
- 1 small glass (5 fluid ounces) low-fat strawberry milk shake: 90 calories
- ½ pomegranate: 55 calories
- 1 sesame rice cake with 1½ teaspoons (¼ oz) tahini: 74 calories
- 3 ounces cooked chicken breasts: 98 calories
- 1 slice of fruit loaf: 98 calories
- ¼ cup (2 ounces) mashed avocado flesh sprinkled with lime juice: 100 calories
- 3½ tablespoons (2 ounces) reduced-fat hummus with cucumber sticks: 100 calories
- 1 package of chees-flavor corn puffs: 96 calories
- 1 package of baked cheese-flavor corn puffs: 83 calories
- 1 slice of garlic bread: 95 calories
- 1 container of fat-free yogurt drink with live cultures and 1 apple (100 g/3½ oz): 78 calories
- 5 small strawberries topped with 2 rounded tablespoons (2½ ounces) of nonfat Greek yogurt with honey: 83 calories
- 1 fish stick with a serving of ketchup: 80 calories
- 1 mini Gouda-type cheese: 61 calories
- 2 water crackers or 1 matzo cracker spread with 1 tablespoon of squeezy guacamole: 84 calories
- 2 cups (1½ oz) arugula dressed with 2 tablespoons of low-fat balsamic dressing and 2 tablespoons (⅓ oz) freshly grated Parmesan cheese: 71 calories
- ½ cup (1½ ounces) marinated olives: 85 calories
- 1 individual package mini rye crispbreads: 90 calories
- 2 clementines and 1 kiwi: 73 calories
- Half a slice of toast cut into strips to dip into 3 tablespoons (2 ounces) mild salsa: 66 calories
- 1 hard-boiled egg: 84 calories
- 2 pieces (2½ ounces) sun-dried tomatoes in oil, drained, on a bed of salad greens: 87 calories
- ¼ cup (1 ounce) unshelled pistachio nuts: 86 calories
- 1 medium orange: 59 calories

- 1-ounce piece of Edam cheese: 85 calories
- 1 large rectangular graham cracker: 59 calories
- 1¼ cups g (10 ounces) shore-bought fresh carrot and cilantro soup: 89 calories
- 1½ ounces canned tuna in water mashed with 3 tablespoons (1 ounce) canned corn kernels and 1 teaspoon of reduced-fat mayonnaise: 92 calories
- 1 store-bought frozen pancake: 92 calories

50 snacks up to 50 calories

- ½ cup (3 ounces) mango cubes: 46 calories
- 1 teaspoon of peanut butter spread on a celery stick: 42 calories
- 1 slice of cantaloupe: 23 calories
- cup (3½ ounces) frozen berries with sweetener: 30 calories
- 1 (3-ounce) apple-and-grape snack container: 45 calories
- 3 seafood sticks: 50 calories
- 2 clementines: 44 calories
- 1 large (3 ounces) whole carrot: 28 calories
- 1 small apple: 42 calories (3½ ounces whole)
- 3 (1 ounce) dried apricots: 38 calories
- ⅔ cup (3½ ounces) fresh blackberries: 25 calories
- ½ cup (2½ ounces) fresh unpitted cherries: 23 calories
- 2 ounces cooked jumbo shrimp with a squeeze of lemon: 42 calories
- 1 gingersnap cookie: 47 calories
- 1 mini light Gouda-type cheese: 42 calories
- 2 slices of wafer-thin ham wrapped around a celery stick: 43 calories
- 2 vanilla wafer cookies: 38 calories
- 1 oat or rice cake with yeast extract: 37 calories
- 1 cup (3½ ounces) cucumber with 3 tablespoons (2 ounces) salsa from a jar: 26 calories
- ⅓ cup (2 ounces) red seedless grapes: 30 calories
- 6 (3½ ounces) cherry tomatoes: 20 calories
- 2 party-size chicken satay skewers: 36 calories
- 2 tablespoons (1 oounce) garlic and herb light cream cheese with celery sticks: 48 calories
- 1 envelope of miso soup with tofu: 30 calories
- ¼ cup (2 ounces) cottage cheese with fruit topping: 47 calories
- 1 rounded tablespoon (1 ounce) of store-bought vegetable couscous salad: 48 calories
- Half a slice of Danish whole-wheat toast spread with 2 teaspoons of salmon paste: 45 calories
- 2 fresh apricots: 33 calories
- 1 water cracker topped with ⅓ ounce French chèvre: 65 calories
- 2 Melba toasts spread with 1 level teaspoon of reduced-sugar preserves: 34 calories
- 6 (3½ ounces) asparagus spears, steamed, with a shake of dried red pepper flakes: 28 calories
- 2 tablespoons of squeezy guacamole with celery sticks: 32 calories
- ½ medium banana: 47 calories
- ½ (3½-ounce) container store-bought vanilla pudding: 45 calories
- 1 small bite-size sausage: 26 calories
- 1 hard-boiled egg, no yolk: 17 calories
- 1 regular cheese triangle: 43 calories
- 1½ cups (1½ ounces) bistro salad (mâche, beet, and Swiss chard) from a bag with 2½ tablespoons (½ ounce) pitted black olives and 1 tablespoon of low-fat French dressing: 41 calories
- 2 cheddar cheese crackers: 44 calories
- 1 nectarine: 45 calories
- ½ pink grapefruit, with sweetener, if desired: 24 calories
- 1 cheese oat or rice cake: 39 calories
- ½ red or orange bell pepper, cut into strips: 26 calories
- 2 teaspoons toasted sunflower seeds: 42 calories
- 1 jumbo cheese-flavor rice and corn cake: 38 calories
- 6 slices (1 ounce) of bresaola: 48 calories
- 4 teaspoons (¾ ounce) relish with carrot sticks: 48 calories
- 1 mini pork salami sausage: 38 calories
- 2 prunes: 39 calories
- ⅔ cup (3½ ounces) papaya flesh: 43 calories

Recipes

Some of the recipes in this book are for just one person, while others serve two, four, or more. If you are the only one doing 5:2 in your household, you may naturally gravitate more to the ones that are single servings. However, from the feedback we've had, many couples are doing intermittent fasting together and so will love to find recipes that serve two. We've also included recipes that, despite being low in calories, taste delicious and work well for all the family or a group of adults. If you are the chief cook, not having to make a separate dish for yourself can help both practically and psychologically toward your 5:2 success. Needless to say, it is important to always only serve yourself the correct amount, and not to go back for seconds. Any of the recipes in this book can also easily be modified by multiplying or dividing ingredients as appropriateÒ—for example doubling the ingredients to make a "for one" recipe suitable for a couple, or halving or dividing the ingredients of a recipe for four to make it suitable for two or one. Alternatively, most leftovers will keep safely in the refrigerator for at least 48 hours.

Fruity summer milk shake

PREPARATION TIME **2 MINUTES**

89
CALORIES
PER SERVING

SERVES
1

- ½ ripe peach, halved, pitted, and chopped
- ½ cup halved or quartered hulled strawberries
- ⅔ cup raspberries
- scant ½ cup milk
- ice cubes, to serve

Put the peach, strawberries, and raspberries in a blender or food processor and blend to a smooth puree, scraping the mixture down from the sides of the bowl, if necessary.

Add the milk and blend the ingredients again until the mixture is smooth and frothy. Pour the milk shake over the ice cubes in 2 tall glasses. Serve immediately.

Cranberry yogurt smoothie

PREPARATION TIME **3—4 MINUTES**

113
CALORIES
PER SERVING

SERVES
2

- 2 medium apples
- 1 cup frozen cranberries
- ½ cup low-fat plain yogurt
- 1 tablespoon honey
- ice cubes, to serve

Juice the apples, then place the juice in a blender or food processor with the remaining ingredients and blend until smooth. Pour the smoothie over ice cubes in glasses. Serve immediately.

Prune & banana crunch

PREPARATION TIME **5 MINUTES**

274
CALORIES
PER SERVING

SERVES
2

- 1 firm, ripe banana, diced
- 10 pitted prunes
- 1 cup nonfat Greek yogurt
- 1½ cups cornflakes or crunchy cereal flakes

Mix together the banana, prunes, and yogurt in a large bowl.

Spoon into 2 glass serving bowls and top with the cornflakes or crunchy cereal flakes. Serve immediately.

Spiced apple millet porridge

PREPARATION TIME **1 MINUTES** • COOKING TIME **3–4 MINUTES**

174
CALORIES
PER SERVING

SERVES
1

- 1 cup apple juice
- ½ teaspoon ground cinnamon
- ⅔ cup millet flakes

To serve
- 1 tablespoon nonfat Greek yogurt
- demerara or other raw sugar (optional)

Put the apple juice and cinnamon in a microwaveable serving bowl. Sprinkle in the millet flakes and stir gently.

Microwave on full power for 3–4 minutes, stirring frequently, until thick and creamy. Alternatively, put the ingredients in a small saucepan and heat gently for 6–8 minutes, stirring frequently, until thick and creamy. Add a little extra juice if the mixture becomes dry. Serve hot with a tablespoon of yogurt and, if you like your porridge sweet, a teaspoon of sugar (remembering to count the calories).

Apple & yogurt muesli

PREPARATION TIME **10 MINUTES, PLUS SOAKING**

303 CALORIES PER SERVING

SERVES **2**

- 1 cup fruit and nut muesli, preferably without added sugar
- 1 crisp apple, such as Pippin or Golden Delicious, peeled and coarsely grated
- 1 cup chilled apple juice
- ½ cup nonfat Greek yogurt with honey

To serve
- flaxseeds (optional)
- honey (optional)

Put the muesli in a bowl and mix with the apples. Pour the apple juice over the cereal, stir well to combine, and let soak for 5–6 minutes.

Divide the soaked muesli among 2 serving bowls and spoon the yogurt on top. Sprinkle with the flaxseeds, if using, and serve with a drizzle of honey, if desired (remembering to count the calories).

Maple-glazed granola

PREPARATION TIME **20 MINUTES, PLUS COOLING** • COOKING TIME **7–10 MINUTES**

246 CALORIES PER SERVING

SERVES **3**

- **1 tablespoon olive oil**
- **1 tablespoon maple syrup**
- **¼ cup slivered almonds**
- **2½ tablespoons pine nuts**
- **1½ tablespoons sunflower seeds**
- **2½ tablespoons rolled oats**
- **¾ cup plain yogurt**

Fruit salad

- **½ mango, peeled, pitted, and sliced**
- **1 kiwi, peeled and sliced**
- **handful of red seedless grapes, halved**
- **grated rind and juice of ½ lime**

Heat the oil in a flameproof skillet with a metal handle, add the maple syrup, nuts, seeds, and oats, and toss together.

Transfer the skillet to a preheated oven, at 350°F, and cook for 5–8 minutes, stirring once and moving the brown edges to the center, until the granola mixture is evenly toasted. Let cool. (The cooled granola can be stored in a sealed jar for up to 10 days.)

To make the fruit salad, mix together the fruits and lime rind and juice in a bowl, then divide among 3 dishes. Spoon the yogurt on top, sprinkle with the granola, and serve.

TOP TIP

Make a list of the reasons why you are fasting and stick it on front of your refrigerator. This will remind you of your goals whenever you reach for something to eat!

Blueberry bran muffins

PREPARATION TIME **10 MINUTES** • COOKING TIME **18–20 MINUTES**

142 CALORIES PER SERVING

SERVES 12

- 2 cups all-purpose flour
- ¾ cup rice bran
- 1 teaspoon baking powder
- 1 teaspoon baking soda
- 3 eggs
- 1 teaspoon vanilla extract
- 1 cup buttermilk
- ¼ cup peanut or sunflower oil, plus extra for greasing
- ¾ cup blueberries

Mix together the dry ingredients in a large bowl until well combined. Lightly beat the eggs in a small bowl, then stir in the vanilla extract, buttermilk, and oil.

Pour the wet ingredients into the dry ingredients, then add the blueberries and fold in gently, using a large metal spoon, until only just combined.

Using a large metal spoon, divide the batter between the cups of a lightly oiled 12-cup muffin pan or a 12-cup muffin pan lined with paper liners.

Bake in a preheated oven, at 350°F, for 18–20 minutes, until risen, golden brown, and firm. Transfer to a wire rack to cool slightly before serving warm.

Cranberry muffins

PREPARATION TIME **10 MINUTES** • COOKING TIME **18–20 MINUTES**

172 CALORIES PER SERVING · SERVES **12**

- 2½ cups all-purpose flour
- 4 teaspoons baking powder
- ⅓ cup firmly packed light brown sugar
- 3 pieces of preserved ginger from a jar (about 2 ounces), finely chopped
- ⅔ cup dried cranberries
- 1 egg
- 1 cup milk
- ¼ cup vegetable oil

Sift the flour and baking powder into a large bowl, then stir in the sugar, ginger, and cranberries until well combined. Beat together the egg, milk, and oil in a small bowl.

Pour the wet ingredients into the dry ingredients, then stir gently, using a large metal spoon, until only just combined. The batter should look craggy, with specks of flour still visible.

Using a large metal spoon, divide the batter among the cups of a 12-cup muffin pan lined with paper liners, piling it up in the centers.

Bake in a preheated oven, at 400°F, for 18–20 minutes, until well risen and golden brown. Transfer to a wire rack to cool slightly before serving warm.

Pistachio & date squares

PREPARATION TIME **10 MINUTES, PLUS COOLING AND CHILLING** • COOKING TIME **20 MINUTES**

171 CALORIES PER SERVING

SERVES 20

- grated rind of 1 lemon
- ½ cup chopped dried dates
- ½ cup unsalted pistachio nuts, chopped
- ¾ cup slivered almonds, chopped
- ⅔ cup firmly packed light brown sugar
- 3¾ cups millet flakes
- 1⅓ cups cornflakes, lightly crushed
- 1 (14-ounce) can condensed milk
- 2 tablespoons mixed seeds, such as pumpkin and sunflower

Mix together all the ingredients in a large bowl, then spoon into an 11 x 7-inch baking pan and spread evenly.

Place in a preheated oven, at 350°F, for 20 minutes. Let cool in the pan, then mark into 20 squares and chill until firm.

TOP TIP

To prepare for your fast day, shop in advance for all the ingredients you will need and try to make sure that there are no tempting snacks on hand that might lead you astray.

Moroccan baked eggs

170 CALORIES PER SERVING

SERVES **2**

- ½ tablespoon olive oil
- ½ onion, chopped
- 1 garlic clove, sliced
- ½ teaspoon ras el hanout
- pinch ground cinnamon
- ½ teaspoon ground coriander
- 2¾ cups cherry tomatoes
- 2 tablespoons chopped fresh cilantro
- 2 eggs
- salt and black pepper

Heat the oil in a skillet over medium heat, add the onion and garlic, and cook for 6–7 minutes or until softened and lightly golden brown, stirring occasionally. Stir in the spices and cook for another 1 minute. Add the tomatoes and season well with salt and black pepper, then simmer gently for 8–10 minutes.

Sprinkle with 1 tablespoon of the cilantro, then divide the tomato mixture between 2 individual ovenproof dishes. Break an egg into each dish.

Bake in a preheated oven, at 425°F, for 8–10 minutes, until the egg is set but the yolks are still slightly runny. Cook for another 2–3 minutes if you prefer the eggs to be cooked through. Serve sprinkled with the remaining cilantro.

Ham & tomato omelets

PREPARATION TIME **20 MINUTES** • COOKING TIME **30 MINUTES**

278 CALORIES PER SERVING

SERVES 4

- 4 teaspoons extra virgin canola oil
- 4 shallots, thinly sliced
- 8 eggs, lightly beaten
- 2 tablespoons chopped fresh mixed herbs, such as chives, chervil, parsley, basil, and thyme
- 12 yellow and red cherry tomatoes, halved
- 5 ounces wafer-thin smoked ham slices
- salt and black pepper

Heat 1 teaspoon of the oil in a medium skillet over medium-low heat, add the shallots, and cook gently for 4–5 minutes or until softened.

Meanwhile, beat together the eggs and herbs in a small bowl and season with salt and black pepper.

Remove three-quarters of the shallots from the skillet with a slotted spoon and set aside. Pour one-quarter of the egg mixture into the skillet, then sprinkle one-quarter of the cherry tomatoes over the egg mixture and stir gently, using a heat-resistant rubber spatula, until the egg is almost set. Spread one-quarter of the sliced ham evenly over the top of the omelet and cook gently for another 1 minute.

Fold the omelet in half, slide out of the skillet onto a warm plate, and serve immediately. Repeat with the remaining ingredients to make another 3 omelets. Alternatively, keep the cooked omelets warm until all 4 are ready and serve at the same time.

Red pepper & ginger soup

PREPARATION TIME **20 MINUTES, PLUS COOLING** • COOKING TIME **45 MINUTES**

112 CALORIES PER SERVING

SERVES **2**

- 1½ **red bell peppers, quartered, cored,and seeded**
- ½ **red onion, quartered**
- 1 **garlic clove, unpeeled**
- ½ **teaspoon olive oil**
- 1-inch **piece of fresh ginger root, peeled and grated**
- ½ **teaspoon ground cumin**
- ½ **teaspoon ground coriander**
- 1 **medium potato, peeled and chopped**
- 2 **cups vegetable stock**
- **salt and black pepper**
- 2 **tablespoons low-fat fromage blanc, sour cream, or Greek yogurt, to serve**

Put the bell peppers, onion, and garlic into a nonstick roasting pan. Roast in a preheated oven, at 400°F, for 40 minutes or until the bell peppers have blistered and the onion and garlic are soft. If the onion quarters start to brown too much, cover them with the bell pepper halves.

Meanwhile, heat the oil in a saucepan, add the ginger, cumin, and coriander, and cook over low heat for 1–2 minutes or until softened. Add the potato, stir well, and season with salt and bell pepper, then pour in the stock. Cover and simmer for 30 minutes.

Remove the vegetables from the oven. Place the bell peppers in a plastic bag, tie the top, and let cool. (The steam produced in the bag makes it easier to remove the skin when the peppers are cool.) Add the onions to the potato mixture and carefully squeeze out the garlic pulp into the saucepan. Peel the peppers and add all but one-quarter to the soup. Simmer for 5 minutes.

Transfer the soup to a blender or food processor and blend until smooth. Alternatively, rub the soup through a strainer to puree. Return the soup to the pan and thin with a little water, if necessary. Heat through gently.

Slice the remaining black pepper. Ladle the soup into 2 warm bowls and arrange pepper slices on top of each with a spoonful of fromage blanc, sour cream, or Greek yogurt.

Ginger & parsnip soup

PREPARATION TIME **10 MINUTES** • COOKING TIME **20 MINUTES**

151 CALORIES PER SERVING

SERVES **2**

- **1 tablespoon butter**
- **¼ cup peeled and thinly sliced fresh ginger root**
- **½ bunch of scallions**
- **2 medium parsnips, peeled and sliced**
- **2½ cups vegetable stock**
- **salt and black pepper**

Melt the butter in a saucepan, add the ginger, and sauté gently for 1 minute. Reserve ½ a scallion. Coarsely chop the remainder and add to the pan with the parsnips. Cook gently for 2 minutes.

Add the stock and bring to a boil. Reduce the heat, cover, and simmer gently for 15 minutes, until the parsnips are tender.

Meanwhile, shred the reserved scallion lengthwise into fine ribbons.

Transfer the soup to a blender or food processor and blend until smooth. Alternatively, blend in the pan using an immersion blender. Return the soup to the pan, if necessary, season with salt and black pepper, and heat through gently for 1 minute. Serve the soup sprinkled with the scallion ribbons.

Coconut & butternut soup

PREPARATION TIME **10 MINUTES** • COOKING TIME **25 MINUTES**

120 CALORIES PER SERVING

SERVES **6**

- 1 tablespoon olive oil
- 1 onion, chopped
- 1 garlic clove, crushed
- 2 butternut squashes, peeled, seeded, and cubed
- 2 teaspoons medium curry paste
- 2½ cups vegetable stock
- 1 cup reduced-fat coconut milk
- 2 tablespoons chopped cilantro

Heat the oil in a large saucepan, add the onion and garlic, and sauté for 4–5 minutes, until softened. Add the squash and sauté for 1 minute, then stir in the curry paste and cook for another 1 minute.

Pour in the stock and bring to a boil, then reduce the heat, cover, and simmer for 15 minutes, until the squash is tender.

Transfer the soup to a blender or food processor and blend until smooth. Return the soup to the pan, stir in the coconut milk and cilantro, and season with salt and black pepper. Heat through gently before serving.

Quick & easy miso soup

PREPARATION TIME **5 MINUTES** • COOKING TIME **10 MINUTES**

58 CALORIES PER SERVING

SERVES **2**

- 2 cups vegetable stock
- 1 tablespoon miso paste
- 2 ounces shiitake mushrooms, sliced
- 4 ounces tofu, cubed

Pour the stock into a saucepan and heat until simmering.

Add the miso paste, shiitake mushrooms, and tofu to the stock and simmer for 5 minutes. Ladle the soup into 2 warm bowls and serve.

Hot & sour mushroom soup

PREPARATION TIME **5 MINUTES** • COOKING TIME **15 MINUTES**

23 CALORIES PER SERVING

SERVES **4**

- **5 cups fish stock**
- **1 lemon grass stalk, lightly crushed**
- **3 fresh kaffir lime leaves or 3 pieces of lime rind**
- **2 Thai red chiles, halved and seeded**
- **2 tablespoons lime juice**
- **2 tablespoons Thai fish sauce**
- **⅓ cup canned bamboo shoots**
- **4 ounces oyster mushrooms**
- **2 scallions, finely sliced**
- **½ red chile, sliced, to garnish**

Pour the stock into a saucepan and add the lemon grass, lime leaves or rind, and chiles. Simmer for 10 minutes.

Strain the liquid into a clean saucepan. Reserve a little red chile and discard the remaining seasonings. Add the lime juice and fish sauce to the soup with the bamboo shoots and mushrooms and reserved chile.

Simmer the soup for 5 minutes, then ladle into 4 warm bowls and sprinkle with the scallions. Serve garnished with red chile slices.

Hot & sour shrimp soup

282 CALORIES PER SERVING

SERVES 4

- 4 cups light and clear chicken or vegetable broth
- 3 tablespoons Thai fish sauce
- 1 tablespoon rice wine vinegar
- 1 tablespoon lime juice
- 1 tablespoon palm sugar or packed light brown sugar
- 1 garlic clove, sliced
- 1 red chile, thinly sliced
- 3 kaffir lime leaves
- 2 teaspoons tamarind paste
- 7 ounces rice vermicelli
- 8 baby corn, sliced
- 8 ounces raw, peeled jumbo shrimp
- 1 cup bean sprouts
- 2 tablespoons shredded mint

Pour the stock into a large saucepan and add the fish sauce, vinegar, lime juice, sugar, garlic, chile, lime leaves, and tamarind paste. Bring to a boil over medium-high heat, then reduce the heat and simmer gently for 12 minutes.

Meanwhile, put the rice vermicelli in a bowl of boiling water and let stand for 2–3 minutes, until tender, or cook according to the package directions. Drain well and divide among 4 warm, deep serving bowls.

Stir the baby corn into the broth and simmer for 2 minutes, then add the shrimp and simmer for another 2–3 minutes, until the shrimp turn pink and are just cooked through.

Ladle the broth over the vermicelli, then sprinkle with the bean sprouts and mint and serve immediately.

Fragrant soba noodle soup

PREPARATION TIME **10 MINUTES** • COOKING TIME **12–14 MINUTES**

314 CALORIES PER SERVING

SERVES **4**

- 5 cups clear chicken or vegetable stock
- 1 lemon grass stalk, finely sliced
- 1-inch piece of fresh ginger root, peeled and finely chopped
- 3 lime leaves, thinly sliced
- 1 small red chile, seeded and finely sliced (optional)
- 1 tablespoon Thai fish sauce
- 8 ounces buckwheat soba noodles
- 7 ounces firm tofu, diced
- 1 scallion, thinly sliced
- 2 tablespoons chopped cilantro

Pour the stock into a saucepan and add the lemon grass, ginger, lime leaves, chile, if using, and fish sauce. Bring to a boil, then reduce the heat to low and simmer gently for 10–12 minutes.

Meanwhile, bring a large saucepan of water to a boil and cook the noodles for 6–7 minutes, or according to the package directions, until tender. Drain the noodles and divide among 4 warm serving bowls.

Spread the tofu over the noodles and then carefully ladle over the hot soup. Sprinkle with the scallion and cilantro and serve immediately.

Butternut & rosemary soup

PREPARATION TIME **15 MINUTES** • COOKING TIME **1 HOUR 10 MINUTES**

146 CALORIES PER SERVING

SERVES 4

- 1 butternut squash, halved, seeded, and cut into small chunks
- a few rosemary sprigs, plus extra leaves to garnish
- ¾ cup dried red lentils, washed and drained
- 1 onion, finely chopped
- 3¾ cups vegetable stock
- salt and black pepper

Place the squash pieces in a nonstick roasting pan. Sprinkle the rosemary over the squash and season with salt and black pepper. Roast in a preheated oven, at 400°F, for 45 minutes.

Meanwhile, put the lentils in a saucepan and cover with water, then bring to a boil and boil rapidly for 10 minutes. Drain, then return to a clean saucepan with the onion and stock and simmer for 5 minutes. Season with salt and black pepper.

Remove the squash from the oven and scoop the flesh from the skin. Mash the flesh with a fork and add it to the soup, then simmer for 25 minutes, until the lentils are tender. Serve the soup sprinkled with extra rosemary.

Lentil & goat cheese salad

PREPARATION TIME **10 MINUTES** • COOKING TIME **20–30 MINUTE**

250 CALORIES PER SERVING

SERVES **2**

- 1 teaspoon olive oil
- 1 teaspoon cumin seeds
- 1 garlic clove, crushed
- 1 teaspoon peeled and grated fresh ginger root
- ¼ cup green lentils
- 1½ cups hot chicken or vegetable stock
- 1 tablespoon chopped mint
- 1 tablespoon chopped cilantro
- squeeze of lime juice
- 3 cups baby spinach leaves
- 2 ounces goat cheese, crumbled
- black pepper

Heat the oil in a saucepan over medium heat, add the cumin seeds, garlic, and ginger, and cook for 1 minute. Add the lentils and cook for another 1 minute.

Pour the stock into the pan one ladleful at a time, waiting until the liquid has been absorbed before adding more, and cook for about 10–20 minutes, until the lentils are tender. Remove the pan from the heat and stir in the herbs and lime juice.

Divide the spinach leaves among 2 serving bowls, top with the lentils and goat cheese, and sprinkle with black pepper.

TOP TIP

Watch out for condiments. Replace ketchup, mayonnaise, or salad dressing with balsamic vinegar, mustard, or lemon juice, which have fewer calories.

Vietnamese-style noodle salad

PREPARATION TIME **20 MINUTES** • COOKING TIME **4 MINUTES**

271 CALORIES PER SERVING

SERVES 4

- **7 ounces fine rice noodles**
- **½ cucumber, seeded and cut into matchsticks**
- **1 carrot, cut into matchsticks**
- **1½ cups bean sprouts**
- **2 cups snow peas, cut into thin strips**
- **2 tablespoons chopped cilantro**
- **2 tablespoons chopped mint**
- **1 red chile, seeded and finely sliced**
- **2 tablespoons chopped blanched peanuts, to garnish**

Dressing
- **1 tablespoon peanut or sunflower oil**
- **½ teaspoon sugar**
- **1 tablespoon Thai fish sauce**
- **2 tablespoons lime juice**

Bring a large saucepan of water to a boil, then turn off the heat and add the rice noodles. Cover and let cook for 4 minutes, or according to the package directions, until just tender. Drain the noodles and cool immediately in a bowl of ice-cold water.

Make the dressing by combining all the ingredients in a screw-top jar until the sugar is dissolved.

Drain the noodles and return to the bowl. Pour over half of the dressing, then add the vegetables, herbs, and chile. Toss until well combined.

Pile the noodle salad onto 4 serving plates and drizzle with the remaining dressing. Serve sprinkled with the chopped peanuts.

Spiced chicken & mango salad

PREPARATION TIME **15 MINUTES** • COOKING TIME **5–6 MINUTES**

221 CALORIES PER SERVING — SERVES **2**

- 3 teaspoons mild curry paste
- juice of ½ lemon
- 2 small boneless, skinless chicken breasts, cut into long, thin strips
- ⅓ cup low-fat plain yogurt
- ½ bunch watercress, torn into pieces
- ¼ cucumber, diced
- ¼ red onion, chopped
- ½ mango, peeled, pitted, and cut into chunks
- ¼ iceberg lettuce, torn into pieces

Put 2 teaspoons of the curry paste in a plastic bag with the lemon juice and mix together by squeezing the bag. Add the chicken and toss together.

Arrange the chicken in a single layer in a steamer set over a large saucepan of boiling water, cover, and cook for 5–6 minutes or until cooked through.

Meanwhile, mix the remaining curry paste in a bowl with the yogurt. Add the watercress, cucumber, red onion, and mango to the yogurt dressing and gently toss together.

Divide the lettuce between 2 serving plates, spoon the mango mixture over the leaves, and top with the warm chicken strips. Serve immediately.

Grilled chicken salad

PREPARATION TIME **10 MINUTES** • COOKING TIME **10 MINUTES**

298 CALORIES PER SERVING

SERVES 2

- **2 boneless chicken breasts, about 4 ounces per breast**
- **½ tablespoon olive oil**
- **¼ cup cooked pearl barley**
- **½ red onion, finely chopped**
- **½ red chile, finely chopped**
- **2 tablespoons chopped cilantro**
- **grated rind and juice of 1 lime**
- **½ red bell pepper, cored, seeded, and finely chopped**
- **salt and black pepper**
- **parsley sprigs, to garnish**
- **lime wedges, to serve**

Brush each chicken breast with a little oil. Heat a ridged grill pan until hot, add the chicken, and cook for 4–5 minutes on each side or until cooked through and browned. Cut each breast into 4 slices.

Put the barley in a large bowl and stir in the remaining oil. Add the remaining ingredients, season with salt and black pepper, and stir to combine.

Spoon the barley onto 2 serving plates, top with the grilled chicken, and garnish with sprigs of parsley. Serve with lime wedges.

TOP TIP

It's possible to confuse hunger with thirst so, when you feel hungry, try drinking a large glass of water. To stay healthy and hydrated throughout the day, it is important to drink plenty of water.

Italian broccoli & egg salad

PREPARATION TIME **10 MINUTES** • COOKING TIME **5 MINUTES**

198 CALORIES PER SERVING

SERVES **2**

- ¼ head broccoli
- 1 leek, trimmed and thickly sliced
- 2 hard-boiled eggs

Dressing
- 2 tablespoons lemon juice
- 1 tablespoon olive oil
- 1 teaspoon honey
- ½ tablespoon capers, well drained
- 1 tablespoon chopped tarragon, plus extra sprigs to garnish (optional)
- salt and black pepper

Cut the broccoli into florets and thickly slice the stems. Put the broccoli in a steamer set over a saucepan of boiling water, cover, and cook for 3 minutes, then add the leeks and cook for another 2 minutes.

Meanwhile, make the dressing by combining all the ingredients in a salad bowl, then season with salt and black pepper.

Shell and coarsely chop the eggs.

Add the broccoli and leeks to the dressing, toss together, and sprinkle with the chopped eggs. Garnish with tarragon sprigs, if desired, and serve warm.

Shiitake mushroom omelet

PREPARATION TIME **5 MINUTES** • COOKING TIME **5 MINUTES**

270 CALORIES PER SERVING

SERVES **2**

- 2 teaspoons sesame oil
- 4 ounces shiitake mushrooms, sliced
- 3 tablespoons chopped chives, plus extra to garnish
- 1 teaspoon miso paste
- ¼ cup boiling water
- 5 eggs, lightly beaten
- black pepper

Heat the oil in a skillet over medium heat, add the mushrooms and chives, and sauté for 2 minutes.

Dissolve the miso in a boiling water and add to the skillet. Continue to cook until the liquid has evaporated.

Pour the eggs over the mushroom mixture and swirl around the skillet to form a thin omelet. Cook for 1 minute.

Remove the omelet from the heat and slide onto a plate. Roll up and sprinkle with black pepper and a few extra chives. Cut in half, place on 2 serving plates, and serve hot.

TOP TIP

Keep a record of everything you eat and drink in a food journal. This is a good way to make sure that you are staying within you calorie limit while still eating a balanced diet.

Baked portobello mushrooms

42 CALORIES PER SERVING

SERVES **2**

- 2½ large portabello or open cap mushrooms
- 2 tablespoons balsamic vinegar
- ½ tablespoon whole-grain mustard
- ¾ bunch watercress
- salt and black pepper
- Parmesan cheese shavings, to serve (optional)

Remove and reserve the stems from 2 of the mushrooms. Place the 2 mushrooms, skin side down, in a small nonstick roasting pan and bake in a preheated oven, at 400°F, for 15 minutes.

Meanwhile, make the dressing. Finely chop the remaining half mushroom and the reserved stems and mix them in a small bowl with the vinegar and mustard. Season with salt and black pepper.

Remove the mushrooms from the oven and spoon some dressing over each one. Return to the oven and cook for another 25 minutes, covering the pan with aluminum foil after 10 minutes.

Transfer the mushrooms to a plate and keep warm. Add the watercress to the hot juices and toss well. Spoon piles of watercress onto 2 serving plates. Place a mushroom on each and sprinkle with Parmesan shavings, if using.

Mushroom crepes

PREPARATION TIME **20–25 MINUTES** • COOKING TIME **35 MINUTES**

112 CALORIES PER SERVING

SERVES 4

- ⅓ cup all-purpose flour
- ⅔ cup skim milk
- 1 medium egg, beaten
- 1 teaspoon olive oil
- salt and black pepper
- flat-leaf parsley sprigs, to garnish

Filling
- 10 ounces cremini mushrooms, chopped
- 1 bunch of scallions, finely chopped
- 1 garlic clove, chopped
- 1⅔ cups drained canned diced tomatoes
- 2 tablespoons chopped oregano

Put the flour, milk, egg, and salt and black pepper in a blender or food processor and blend until smooth or beat by hand.

Heat a few drops of oil in a nonstick skillet. Pour in a ladleful of the batter and cook for 1 minute. Carefully flip the thin pancake over and cook the other side. Slide the pancake out of the pan onto wax paper. Make 3 more pancakes in the same way, adding a few more drops of oil to the skillet between each one, and stack the pancakes between sheets of wax paper.

Meanwhile, make the filling. Put all the ingredients in a small saucepan and cook for 5 minutes, stirring occasionally. Divide the filling among the pancakes, reserving a little of the mixture to serve, then roll them up.

Transfer the pancakes to an ovenproof dish and place in a preheated oven, at 350°F, for 20 minutes. Serve with the remaining mushroom mixture and garnish with parsley sprigs.

Basil & tomato stew

PREPARATION TIME **10 MINUTES** • COOKING TIME **15 MINUTES**

228 CALORIES PER SERVING

SERVES **4**

- 8 ripe tomatoes (about 2 pounds)
- 6 tablespoons olive oil
- 2 onions, chopped
- 4 celery sticks, sliced
- 4 plump garlic cloves, thinly sliced
- 3 cups sliced white button mushrooms
- 3 tablespoons tomato paste
- 2½ cups vegetable stock
- 1 tablespoon packed light brown sugar
- 3 tablespoons capers, drained
- large handful of basil leaves (about ½ ounce), torn
- large handful of chervil or flat leaf parsley (about ½ ounce), torn
- salt and black pepper

Put the tomatoes into a large saucepan or heatproof bowl and pour over enough boiling water to cover, then let stand for about 1 minute. Drain, then skin the tomatoes carefully. Quarter and seed the tomatoes, scooping out the pulp into a strainer over a bowl to catch the juices.

Heat ¼ cup of the oil in a large saucepan, add the onions and celery, and sauté for 5 minutes. Add the garlic and mushrooms and sauté for another 3 minutes.

Add the tomatoes and their juices, the tomato paste, stock, sugar, and capers and bring to a boil. Reduce the heat and simmer gently, uncovered, for 5 minutes.

Add the herbs to the pan with a little salt and black pepper and cook for 1 minute. Ladle into 4 serving bowls, drizzle with the remaining oil, and serve.

Butternut squash & ricotta frittata

PREPARATION TIME **10 MINUTES** • COOKING TIME **25–30 MINUTES**

248 CALORIES PER SERVING

SERVES 6

- 1 tablespoon extra virgin canola oil
- 1 red onion, thinly sliced
- 3 cups diced, peeled butternut squash
- 8 eggs
- 1 tablespoon chopped thyme
- 2 tablespoons chopped sage
- ½ cup ricotta cheese
- salt and black pepper

Heat the oil in a large, deep skillet with an ovenproof handle over medium-low heat, add the onion and butternut squash, then cover loosely and cook gently, stirring frequently, for 18–20 minutes or until softened and golden brown.

Lightly beat the eggs, thyme, sage, and ricotta in a small bowl, then season well with salt and black pepper and pour over the squash.

Cook for another 2–3 minutes, until the egg is almost set, stirring occasionally with a heat-resistant rubber spatula to prevent the bottom from burning.

Slide the skillet under a preheated broiler, keeping the handle away from the heat, and broil for 3–4 minutes or until the egg is set and the frittata is golden brown. Slice into 6 wedges and serve hot.

Leek & tomato phyllo tarts

PREPARATION TIME **20 MINUTES, PLUS SOAKING** • COOKING TIME **30 MINUTES**

135 CALORIES PER SERVING • **SERVES 4**

- 8 sun-dried tomatoes
- 2 leeks, trimmed and thinly sliced
- 1¼ cups white wine
- 2 tablespoons skim milk
- 1 medium egg, separated
- ¼ cup low-fat cream cheese
- 12 pieces of phyllo pastry, each about 6 inches square
- salt and black pepper

Put the tomatoes into a small bowl and pour over enough boiling water to cover. Let soak for 20 minutes.

Meanwhile, put the leeks and wine in a saucepan and bring to a boil, then reduce the heat and simmer until the liquid has evaporated. Remove the pan from the heat and stir in the milk, egg yolk, and cheese. Season with salt and black pepper.

Brush a pastry square with a little egg white and use it to line the bottom and sides of a 4-inch tart pan. Brush 2 more squares and lay these on top, each at a slight angle to the first, allowing the edges to flop over the rim. Repeat with the remaining squares to line 3 more tart pans.

Put a spoonful of the cooked leek mixture in each pastry shell. Lay 2 of the rehydrated tomatoes on top of each tart and cover with the remaining leek mixture. Season again and place in a preheated oven, at 400°F, for 20 minutes, covering the tarts with pieces of aluminum foil after 10 minutes. Serve hot.

Red lentil dhal with okra

PREPARATION TIME **5 MINUTES** • COOKING TIME **20 MINUTES**

366 CALORIES PER SERVING

SERVES **4**

- 1 onion, chopped
- 1¼ cups dried red lentils, washed and drained
- 1 teaspoon ground turmeric
- 1 green chile, seeded and sliced
- 2 tablespoons tomato paste
- 3¾ cups vegetable stock
- ⅓ cup grated fresh coconut
- 2 tablespoons peanut or vegetable oil
- 8 ounces okra, trimmed and halved crosswise
- 2 teaspoons cumin seeds
- 1 tablespoon mustard seeds
- 2 teaspoons nigella seeds
- 2 garlic cloves, chopped
- 6 curry leaves (optional)
- salt and black pepper

Put the onion, lentils, turmeric, chile, tomato paste, stock, and grated coconut into a saucepan. Bring to a boil, then reduce the heat and simmer gently, uncovered, for 15 minutes, stirring frequently, until thickened and pulpy.

Meanwhile, heat the oil in a skillet, add the okra, cumin seeds, mustard seeds, nigella seeds, garlic, and curry leaves, if using, and sauté gently for about 5 minutes, until the okra is tender.

Season the lentil dhal with salt and black pepper and serve topped with the spiced okra.

Asparagus with smoked salmon

PREPARATION TIME **10 MINUTES** • COOKING TIME **6 MINUTES**

150 CALORIES PER SERVING

SERVES 6

- 12 trimmed asparagus spears
- 3 tablespoons coarsely chopped hazelnuts
- 4 teaspoons olive oil
- juice of 1 lime
- 1 teaspoon Dijon mustard
- 12 quail eggs
- 8 ounces smoked salmon
- salt and black pepper

Put the asparagus in a steamer set over a saucepan of boiling water, cover, and cook for 5 minutes, until just tender.

Meanwhile, put the nuts in an aluminum foil-lined broiler pan and cook under a preheated broiler until lightly browned. In a bowl, lightly mix together the oil, lime juice, and mustard with salt and black pepper to taste, then stir in the nuts. Keep warm.

Pour water into a saucepan to a depth of 1½ inches and bring to a boil. Lower the eggs into the water with a slotted spoon and cook for 1 minute. Remove the pan from the heat and let the eggs stand for 1 minute. Drain the eggs, then cool under cold running water and drain again.

Tear the salmon into strips and divide among 6 serving plates. Do the same with the asparagus, then halve the quail eggs, leaving the shells on, if desired, and arrange on top. Drizzle with the warm nut dressing and sprinkled with black pepper.

Chile rice noodles

283 CALORIES PER SERVING

SERVES **2**

- 4 teaspoons seasoned rice vinegar
- 1 tablespoon sugar
- 1 teaspoon Thai fish sauce
- 1 tablespoon soy sauce
- 3½ ounces dried rice ribbon noodles
- 1 tablespoon peanut or vegetable oil
- 1 small red chile, seeded and finely shredded
- 1 small red bell pepper, cored, seeded, and finely shredded
- 1 cup snow peas, thinly sliced lengthwise

Mix together the vinegar, sugar, fish sauce, and soy sauce in a nonmetallic bowl and set aside.

Bring a large saucepan of water to a boil, then turn off the heat and add the rice noodles. Cover and let cook for 3–4 minutes, or according to the package directions, until tender.

Meanwhile, heat the oil in a skillet, add the chile, red bell pepper, and snow peas, and sauté for 3 minutes, until softened.

Drain the noodles and add to the skillet with the reserved sauce mixture. Toss together, then serve immediately.

TOP TIP

Find yourself a diet buddy. Dieting together can introduce a little healthy competition and you can encourage each other when the going gets tough.

Thai dressed rolls

272 CALORIES PER SERVING

SERVES 4

- 1 small iceburg lettuce
- 9 ounces tofu, diced
- 1⅔ cups snow peas, shredded lengthwise

Dressing
- 2 tablespoons sesame oil
- 2 tablespoons light soy sauce
- 2 tablespoons lime juice
- 1 tablespoon packed light brown sugar
- 1 Thai chile, seeded and sliced
- 1 garlic clove, crushed
- black pepper

Remove 8 leaves from the lettuce. Fill a large heatproof bowl with boiling water. Add the separated leaves and let stand for 10 seconds. Drain and refresh under cold running water, then drain again thoroughly.

Finely shred the remaining lettuce and toss in a bowl with the tofu and snow peas.

Make the dressing by combining all the ingredients in a screw-top jar. Pour it over the tofu and gently toss together.

Spoon a little mixture onto the center of each blanched lettuce leaf, then roll up. Chill until ready to serve, then divide among 4 serving plates and serve.

Lime & ginger shrimp coleslaw

PREPARATION TIME **15 MINUTES** • COOKING TIME **2–3 MINUTES**

143 CALORIES PER SERVING

SERVES 2

- ¼ napa cabbage or green cabbage, thinly shredded
- 1 carrot, shredded
- 1 cup bean sprouts
- ½ small bunch of cilantro, finely chopped
- 1 scallion, thinly sliced
- 4 ounces raw, peeled jumbo shrimp
- 1 teaspoon Chinese 5-spice powder
- ½ tablespoon peanut oil
- lime wedges, to serve

Dressing
- 1 teaspoon peeled and finely grated fresh ginger root
- 1 tablespoon lime juice
- ½ teaspoon palm sugar or light brown sugar
- 1 tablespoon light soy sauce
- 1½ teaspoons peanut oil

Toss together the cabbage, carrots, bean sprouts, cilantro, and scallion in a large bowl and set aside.

Make the dressing by combining all the ingredients in a screw-top jar and set aside.

Mix together the shrimp and Chinese 5-spice powder in a bowl until the shrimp are well coated. Heat the oil in a wok or skillet over medium-high heat, add the shrimp, and stir-fry for 2–3 minutes or until the shrimp turn pink and are cooked through. Remove from the pan and drain on paper towels.

Pour the dressing over the vegetables and toss together, then pile the coleslaw on 2 serving plates. Spred the shrimp over the coleslaw and serve with lime wedges.

Piri piri shrimp

PREPARATION TIME **15 MINUTES, PLUS MARINATING** • COOKING TIME **5–6 MINUTES**

104 CALORIES PER SERVING

SERVES 6

- 13 ounces raw jumbo shrimp, shell on with heads removed
- chopped parsley, to garnish
- lemon wedges, to serve

Marinade
- 3 tablespoons olive oil
- grated rind and juice of 1 lemon
- 2 teaspoons piri-piri seasoning
- 2 teaspoons tomato paste
- 2 garlic cloves, finely chopped
- salt and black pepper

Put the shrimp in a strainer, rinse under cold running water, and drain well.

Mix together the marinade ingredients in a shallow nonmetallic bowl. Add the shrimp and toss until evenly coated. Cover and let marinate in the refrigerator for at least 2 hours.

Thread the shrimp onto 12 metal skewers through the thickest part of the body and tail. Cook under a preheated broiler for 5–6 minutes, turning once, until the shrimp turn pink and are cooked through.

Serve 2 skewers per person, sprinkled with chopped parsley, with lemon wedges.

Shrimp & mango kebabs

PREPARATION TIME **15 MINUTES, PLUS MARINATING** • COOKING TIME **4 MINUTES**

111 CALORIES PER SERVING

SERVES 4

- 16 raw, peeled large jumbo shrimp
- 1 large mango, peeled, pitted, and cut into 16 bite-size pieces
- undressed salad, to serve

Marinade
- 1 tablespoon sunflower oil
- ¼ cup lemon juice
- 2 garlic cloves, crushed
- 1 teaspoon peeled and grated fresh ginger root
- 1 teaspoon chili powder
- 1 tablespoon honey
- 1 teaspoon sea salt

Mix together the marinade ingredients in a nonmetallic bowl. Add the shrimp and mix well. Let marinate for about 10 minutes.

Thread 2 shrimp and 2 pieces of mango alternately onto each of 8 presoaked wooden skewers. Place the skewers on an aluminum foil-lined broiler rack, brush with the remaining marinade, and cook under a preheated hot broiler for 2 minutes on each side or until the shrimp turn pink and are cooked through.

Arrange some undressed salad on 4 serving plates and top each with 2 skewers. Serve hot.

TOP TIP

Try having an early night if you feel very hungry at the end of a fast day. Then you can go to sleep safe in the knowledge that you can have a hearty breakfast first thing in the morning.

Jumbo shrimp with pancetta

PREPARATION TIME **5 MINUTES** • COOKING TIME **7–8 MINUTES**

187 CALORIES PER SERVING

SERVES **2**

- ½ teaspoon olive oil
- ½ tablespoon unsalted butter
- 1 ounce pancetta or smoked bacon, finely chopped
- 8 ounces raw, peeled jumbo shrimp
- grated rind and juice of ½ lemon
- 1 small bunch watercress

Heat the oil and butter in a large skillet, add the pancetta or smoked bacon, and sauté for 3–4 minutes, until crisp.

Add the shrimp and sauté for 1 minute on each side or until they turn pink. Sprinkle the lemon rind and juice over the shrimp and sauté for another 1 minute, then add the watercress and combine well. Serve hot.

Salt & pepper squid

PREPARATION TIME **15 MINUTES** • COOKING TIME **6–8 MINUTES**

272 CALORIES PER SERVING

SERVES 4

- **1 pound squid tubes, 4–5 inches long, cleaned**
- **½ teaspoon Sichuan peppercorns, crushed**
- **¼ teaspoon black peppercorns, crushed**
- **½ teaspoon sea salt**
- **¼ cup sunflower oil**
- **1 medium-strength red chile, seeded and thinly sliced**

Salad
- **½ cucumber, peeled**
- **1 bunch watercress**
- **2 scallions, shredded**
- **2 tablespoons dark soy sauce**
- **2 tablespoons sesame oil**
- **2 teaspoons sugar**

To make the salad, cut the cucumber into long, fine strips and toss with the watercress and scallions. Mix the soy sauce, sesame oil, and sugar in a small bowl.

Halve each squid lengthwise to form 2 flat triangles. Using the tip of a small, sharp knife, score the inner side of each piece, making sure you don't cut right through. Pat the pieces dry on paper towels. Mix together the peppercorns and sea salt.

Heat 2 tablespoons of the oil in a large skillet or wok, add the chile, and sauté for 15–30 seconds, until it begins to color. Drain with a slotted spoon and set aside. Add half the squid and cook for 2–3 minutes or until it starts to brown. Drain with a slotted spoon and set aside. Repeat with the remaining oil and squid.

Return all the squid to the pan and sprinkle with the salt and pepper mixture, stir-frying until evenly coated. Transfer to 4 serving plates and scatter with the fried chile. Divide the salad among the plates and drizzle with the dressing. Serve immediately.

Crab Malabar Hill

PREPARATION TIME **10 MINUTES** • COOKING TIME **5–6 MINUTES**

176 CALORIES PER SERVING

SERVES 2

- 1 tablespoon vegetable oil
- 1½ garlic cloves, finely chopped
- 1 teaspoon peeled and finely chopped fresh ginger root
- 3 scallions, thinly sliced
- 1½ red chiles, seeded and finely sliced
- 10 ounces canned white crabmeat, drained
- grated rind and juice of ½ lime
- 2 tablespoons chopped cilantro
- 1 tablespoon chopped mint
- salt and black pepper
- crisp lettuce leaves, to serve

Heat the oil in a large wok or skillet until hot, then add the garlic, ginger, scallions ,and chiles and stir-fry for 2–3 minutes.

Add the crabmeat, lime rind and juice, cilantro, and mint and stir-fry for another 2–3 minutes, then season with salt and black pepper. Serve hot on crisp lettuce leaves.

TOP TIP

Reward yourself for your successes. Set yourself targets and, once you have reached them, treat yourself to something nice.

Split pea & bell pepper patties

PREPARATION TIME **15 MINUTES, PLUS CHILLING** • COOKING TIME **45–50 MINUTES**

312 CALORIES PER SERVING

SERVES **4**

- 3 cups vegetable stock
- 3 garlic cloves
- 1¼ cups yellow split peas
- olive oil spray
- 2 red bell peppers, halved, cored, and seeded
- 1 yellow bell pepper, halved, cored, and seeded
- 1 red onion, quartered
- 1 tablespoon chopped mint, plus extra leaves to garnish
- 2 tablespoons capers, drained and chopped
- flour, for dusting
- salt and black pepper

Tzatziki
- ½ cucumber, finely chopped
- 1 garlic clove, crushed
- 2 tablespoons chopped mint
- 1¼ cups low-fat plain yogurt

Bring the stock to a boil in a large saucepan. Peel and halve 1 of the garlic cloves, then add to the pan with the split peas, and cook for 40 minutes, until the split peas are tender. Season with salt and black pepper and let cool slightly.

Meanwhile, lightly spray a roasting pan with oil. Put the remaining garlic cloves into the pan with the bell peppers and onion and cook in a preheated oven, at 400°F, for 20 minutes. Squeeze the roasted garlic cloves from their skins and chop with the roasted vegetables.

Mix together the split peas, roasted vegetables, mint, and capers in a large bowl. Flour your hands and shape the mixture into 12 patties. Chill until ready to cook.

To make the tzatziki, mix the ingredients together, cover, and chill in the refrigerator for about 30 minutes before serving.

Heat a skillet and spray with oil. Cook the patties, in batches if necessary, for 2 minutes on each side. Serve 3 patties per person, hot or cold, garnished with mint leaves and with a small bowl of tzatziki.

Pea, egg & tofu curry

PREPARATION TIME **10 MINUTES** • COOKING TIME **15 MINUTES**

257 CALORIES PER SERVING

SERVES **4**

- **4 hard-boiled eggs**
- **½ teaspoon ground turmeric**
- **3 tablespoons vegetable oil**
- **1 bay leaf**
- **2 onions, finely chopped**
- **2 garlic cloves, finely chopped**
- **1½ teaspoons ground coriander**
- **1½ teaspoons ground garam masala**
- **½ teaspoon chili powder**
- **1 tablespoon tomato paste**
- **½ cup canned diced tomatoes**
- **½ cup water**
- **4 ounces tofu, cut into ½-inch cubes**
- **1 tablespoon plain yogurt**
- **⅔ cup frozen peas**
- **2 tablespoons finely chopped cilantro**
- **salt and black pepper**

Shell the eggs and coat well in the turmeric. Heat the oil in a large skillet and lightly fry the eggs over a medium heat for 2 minutes, then remove from the pan and set aside.

Add the bay leaf, onions and garlic to the pan and cook over a medium heat for 2 minutes. Stir in the spices and cook for another 1 minute. Add the tomato purée, tomatoes and measurement water, cover and cook for 5 minutes.

Return the eggs to the pan with the tofu, yogurt and peas. Season with a little salt and pepper.

Cook for 5 minutes, then remove the bay leaf, sprinkle with the chopped coriander and serve.

Spicy eggplant curry

PREPARATION TIME **15 MINUTES** • COOKING TIME **20 MINUTES**

231 CALORIES PER SERVING

SERVES 4

- 1 teaspoon cumin seeds
- 4 teaspoons coriander seeds
- 1 teaspoon cayenne pepper
- 2 green chiles, seeded and sliced
- ½ teaspoon ground turmeric
- 4 garlic cloves, crushed
- 1-inch piece of fresh ginger root, peeled and grated
- 1¼ cups warm water
- 1⅔ cups reduced fat coconut milk
- 1 tablespoon tamarind paste
- 1 large eggplant, thinly sliced lengthwise
- salt and black pepper
- 4 mini plain naans or pita breads, to serve

Dry-fry the cumin and coriander seeds in a small, nonstick skillet for a few minutes until aromatic and toasted. Let cool, then crush together.

Mix together the crushed seeds, cayenne, chiles, turmeric, garlic, ginger, and the measured water in a large saucepan and simmer for 10 minutes, until thickened. Season with salt and black pepper, then stir in the coconut milk and tamarind paste.

Arrange the eggplant slices on an aluminum foil-lined broiler rack and brush the tops with some of the curry sauce. Cook under a preheated hot broiler until golden brown.

Stir the eggplant slices into the curry sauce. Serve hot with naan or pita bread.

Squash with red bean sauce

PREPARATION TIME **15 MINUTES** • COOKING TIME **18 MINUTES**

247 CALORIES PER SERVING

SERVES **4**

- 2½ cups vegetable stock
- 2 pounds mixed baby squash, such as butternut or acorn, peeled, quartered, and seeded
- 4 cups baby spinach leaves

Bean sauce
- ¼ cup olive oil
- 4 garlic cloves, thinly sliced
- 1 red bell pepper, cored, seeded, and finely chopped
- 2 tomatoes, chopped
- 1 (15-ounce) can red kidney beans, rinsed and drained
- 1–2 tablespoons hot chili sauce
- small handful of chopped cilantro
- salt

Bring the stock to a boil in a large saucepan, then add the squash. Reduce the heat, cover, and simmer gently for about 15 minutes or until just tender.

Meanwhile, make the sauce. Heat the oil in a skillet, add the garlic and red pepper, and sauté for 5 minutes, stirring frequently, until soft. Add the tomatoes, kidney beans, chili sauce, and a little salt and simmer for 5 minutes, until pulpy.

Drain the squash, reserving the stock, and return to the saucepan. Add the spinach leaves, cover, and cook for about 1 minute, until the spinach has wilted.

Pile the vegetables onto 4 serving plates. Stir ½ cup of the reserved stock into the sauce, and add the cilantro. Spoon the sauce over the vegetables and serve.

Chicken with celeriac cakes

PREPARATION TIME **15 MINUTES** • COOKING TIME **20 MINUTES**

312 CALORIES PER SERVING

SERVES **4**

- 1 head celeriac, peeled
- 1 garlic clove, finely chopped
- 1 small onion, finely chopped
- 2 bacon slices, cut into short strips
- 1 heaping tablespoon walnuts, crushed
- ¼ cup shredded cheddar cheese
- 1 egg white
- 1 tablespoon olive oil
- 4 chicken breasts (about 5 ounces each), with skin on
- salt and black pepper

Sauce
- 1¼ cups apple juice
- ⅔ cup chicken stock
- 1 crisp sweet apple, such as Pippin, peeled and grated

Cut 4 thin, round slices from the celeriac and set aside. Shred the remaining celeriac and combine with the garlic, onion, bacon, and walnuts in a nonstick skillet. Cover and sweat for 4 minutes or until soft.

Remove the skillet from the heat, add the cheese and egg white, and stir to mix thoroughly. Season with salt and black pepper. Divide the mixture into 4 portions and, when cool enough to handle, shape into 4 cakes.

Place the cakes on a nonstick baking sheet and bake in a preheated oven, at 425°F, for 15 minutes or until golden brown.

Meanwhile, brush the reserved celeriac slices with the oil and place on a broiler rack. Season the chicken breasts and place each one, skin side down, on a celeriac slice. Cook under a preheated medium broiler for 4 minutes, then turn the chicken over and cook for another 5–6 minutes or until cooked through.

To make the sauce, pour the apple juice and stock into a saucepan and boil rapidly until reduced by two-thirds. Add the grated apple and remove the pan from the heat.

Transfer the celeriac cakes onto 4 serving plates and top with the chicken breasts. Use paper towels to remove any excess fat from the celeriac slices. Pour a little sauce around the chicken and garnish with the celeriac slices. Serve immediately.

Blackened chicken skewers

PREPARATION TIME **10 MINUTES, PLUS MARINATING** • COOKING TIME **20 MINUTES**

94 CALORIES PER SERVING

SERVES **2**

- **5 ounces boneless, skinless chicken breast, diced**
- **½ tablespoon Cajun seasoning mix**
- **1 tablespoon lemon juice**
- **½ teaspoon olive oil**
- **cilantro sprigs, to garnish**

Put the chicken into a bowl and add the seasoning mix, lemon juice, and oil. Toss well and let marinate for 15 minutes.

Thread the chicken onto 4 presoaked wooden skewers and cover the ends of the skewers with aluminum foil. Cook under a preheated medium broiler for 20 minutes or until cooked through, turning halfway through cooking. Remove the skewers from the broiler and reserve any juices.

Slide the chicken from the skewers onto 2 serving plates, allowing 2 skewers per person, and garnish with sprigs of cilantro. Serve immediately with the juices poured over the skewers.

TOP TIP

If hunger is getting the better of you, try taking a brisk walk around the block or running up and down the stairs five times—anything to take your mind of that grumbling belly.

Lemon & rosemary chicken

PREPARATION TIME **5 MINUTES** • COOKING TIME **25–30 MINUTES**

363 CALORIES PER SERVING

SERVES 4

- **4 chicken breasts (about 5 ounces each), with skin on**
- **2 tablespoons olive oil**
- **1 tablespoon butter**
- **1 rosemary sprig or 1 teaspoon dried rosemary**
- **3 garlic cloves, coarsely sliced**
- **1 cup dry white wine**
- **2 tablespoons lemon juice**
- **5–6 thin strips lemon rind**
- **salt and black pepper**

Rinse the chicken under cold running water and place, skin side down, in a sauté pan. Dry-fry the chicken over medium heat until it is evenly browned on all sides.

Add the oil, butter, rosemary, garlic, and salt and black pepper, then cook for 2–3 minutes, turning the chicken pieces once. Add the wine, increase the heat, and let the wine simmer for about 1 minute.

Reduce the heat to medium-low, cover, and cook for 15–20 minutes or until the chicken is cooked through and still juicy.

Remove the pan from the heat and transfer the chicken to a warm serving dish. Skim the oil off the surface of the liquid, then add the lemon juice and rind and cook over medium heat for 1 minute, stirring gently. Pour the sauce over the chicken and serve.

Carnival chicken

300 CALORIES PER SERVING

SERVES **4**

- **4 skinless chicken breasts (about 5 ounces each)**
- **flat leaf parsley sprigs, to garnish**

Marinade
- **½ cup sweet sherry**
- **1 teaspoon Angostura bitters**
- **1 tablespoon light soy sauce**
- **1 tablespoon peeled and chopped fresh ginger root**
- **pinch of ground cumin**
- **pinch of ground coriander**
- **1 teaspoon dried mixed herbs**
- **1 small onion, finely chopped**
- **⅓ cup chicken stock**

Mashed sweet potatoes
- **3 medium sweet potatoes**
- **salt and black pepper**

Place the chicken breasts in a nonmetallic dish. Mix together the marinade ingredients in a bowl, then spoon it over the chicken, making sure the pieces are well coated. Cover and let marinate in the refrigerator overnight.

Cook the chicken under a preheated medium broiler for 20 minutes or until cooked through, turning halfway through cooking. Remove from the broiler and keep warm.

Meanwhile, boil the sweet potatoes in their skins for 20 minutes until soft. Drain well, then peel. Mash the potatoes and let dry off slightly. Season with salt and black pepper and serve with the chicken, garnished with sprigs of parsley.

Chicken & spinach curry

PREPARATION TIME **10 MINUTES** • COOKING TIME **25 MINUTES**

205 CALORIES PER SERVING

SERVES 4

- 1 tablespoon vegetable oil
- 4 boneless, skinless chicken breasts (about 4 ounces each), halved lengthwise
- 1 onion, sliced
- 2 garlic cloves, chopped
- 1 green chile, chopped
- 4 cardamom pods, lightly crushed
- 1 teaspoon cumin seeds
- 1 teaspoon dried red pepper flakes
- 1 teaspoon ground ginger
- 1 teaspoon ground turmeric
- 8 cups baby spinach leaves
- 1⅔ cups chopped tomatoes
- ⅔ cup low-fat Greek yogurt
- 2 tablespoons chopped cilantro, plus extra sprigs to garnish
- boiled rice, to serve (optional)

Heat the oil in a large skillet or wok, add the chicken, onion, garlic, and chile, and cook for 4–5 minutes or until the chicken begins to brown and the onion to soften. Add the cardamoms, cumin seeds, red pepper flakes, ginger, and turmeric and cook for another 1 minute.

Add the spinach, cover, and cook gently until the spinach wilts, then stir in the tomatoes, replace the cover, and simmer for 15 minutes or until the chicken is cooked through, removing the lid for the last 5 minutes of cooking.

Stir the yogurt and cilantro into the curry and garnished with sprigs of cilantro. Serve with boiled rice, if desired (remembering to count the calories).

Lime & chili chicken kebabs

PREPARATION TIME **15–20 MINUTES, PLUS MARINATING** • COOKING TIME **10 MINUTES**

381 CALORIES PER SERVING

SERVES **2**

- 8 ounces boneless, skinless chicken breasts, cut into strips
- 1 lime, halved
- 3½ ounces rice noodles
- salt and black pepper
- 1 tablespoon chopped cilantro, to garnish

Marinade
- grated rind and juice of 1 lime
- 1 garlic clove, chopped
- 1 tablespoon chopped dried or fresh red chile
- 2 tablespoons sunflower oil

Mix together the marinade ingredients in a nonmetallic bowl. Add the chicken, mix well, and season with salt and black pepper. Cover and let marinate in the refrigerator for 1 hour.

Thread the chicken evenly onto 6 presoaked wooden skewers. Cook the kebabs and lime halves under a preheated hot broiler or in a preheated ridged grill pan for about 10 minutes or until the chicken is cooked through.

Meanwhile, bring a large saucepan of water to a boil, then turn off the heat and add the rice noodles. Cover and let cook for 3–4 minutes, or according to the package directions, until just tender, then drain.

Garnish the chicken with the cilantro and serve 3 skewers per person with the noodles and caramelized lime halves.

Tandoori chicken

175 CALORIES PER SERVING

SERVES **4**

- **4 chicken breasts (about 4½ ounces each)**
- **wine or water**
- **a few herb sprigs, such as rosemary, thyme, or parsley**

Marinade
- **1 tablespoon peeled and grated fresh ginger root**
- **2 teaspoons coriander seeds, toasted**
- **2 teaspoons rosemary leaves**
- **1 teaspoon grated lemon rind**
- **½ teaspoon ground cardamom**
- **½ teaspoon ground cumin**
- **¼ teaspoon crushed black peppercorns**
- **¼ teaspoon chili sauce or powder**
- **½ cup plain yogurt**
- **1 tablespoon lemon juice**

Mix together the marinade ingredients in a bowl. Put the chicken into a nonmetallic dish. Spoon the marinade over the bird and rub well into it. Cover and let marinate in the refrigerator for 2–4 hours.

Scrape the excess marinade from the chicken and discard. Put the chicken onto a wire rack set in a roasting pan. Pour in wine or water to the depth of 1 inch and add the herb sprigs to keep the meat moist during cooking.

Bake the chicken in a preheated oven, at 475°F, for 10 minutes. Turn the chicken over, return to the oven, and bake for another 10 minutes or until cooked through.

Cranberry chicken stir-fry

PREPARATION TIME **15 MINUTES** • COOKING TIME **10 MINUTES**

230 CALORIES PER SERVING

SERVES **4**

- 2 tablespoons vegetable oil
- 2 shallots, finely chopped
- 1-inch piece of fresh ginger root, peeled and thinly sliced into matchsticks
- 2 garlic cloves, crushed
- 10 ounces boneless, skinless chicken breasts, thinly sliced
- 2 tablespoons hoisin sauce
- 2 tablespoons oyster sauce
- 1 tablespoon light soy sauce
- 1 cup dried cranberries
- 4 scallions, diagonally sliced
- 1¼ cups bean sprouts

Basil and chile garnish
- vegetable oil, for deep-frying
- handful of basil leaves
- 1 large red chile, seeded and thinly sliced

Heat the 2 tablespoons oil in a wok or large skillet, add the shallots, ginger, and garlic, and stir-fry over medium heat for 30 seconds. Add the chicken and stir-fry for 2 minutes or until golden brown.

Add the hoisin, oyster, and soy sauces and the cranberries and stir-fry for another 2 minutes, until the chicken is cooked through, then add the scallions and bean sprouts and toss together for 3–4 minutes.

To make the garnish, heat ½ inch of oil in a small saucepan, then deep-fry the basil leaves and red chile, in 2 batches, for 10–30 seconds, until crisp. Remove with a slotted spoon and drain on paper towels.

Serve the stir-fry garnished with the deep-fried basil and chile.

Chicken with spring vegetables

PREPARATION TIME **10 MINUTES, PLUS RESTING** • COOKING TIME **ABOUT 1¼ HOURS**

370 CALORIES PER SERVING

SERVES 4

- 1 (3-pound) chicken
- about 5 cups hot chicken stock
- 2 shallots, halved
- 2 garlic cloves
- 2 parsley sprigs
- 2 marjoram sprigs
- 2 lemon thyme sprigs
- 2 carrots, halved
- 1 leek, trimmed and sliced
- 7 ounces baby broccoli
- 16 asparagus spears, trimmed
- ½ savoy cabbage, shredded

Put the chicken in a large saucepan and pour over enough stock to just cover the chicken. Push the shallots, garlic, herbs, carrots, and leek into the pan and bring to a boil over medium-high heat, then reduce the heat and simmer gently for 1 hour or until the chicken is falling away from the bones.

Add the remaining vegetables to the pan and simmer for another 6–8 minutes or until the vegetables are cooked.

Turn off the heat and let rest for 5–10 minutes. Remove the skin from the chicken, if desired, then divide the chicken among 4 deep serving bowls with the vegetables. Serve with spoonfuls of the broth ladled over the chicken.

Asian steamed chicken salad

PREPARATION TIME 10 MINUTES, PLUS COOLING • COOKING TIME 8–10 MINUTES

273 CALORIES PER SERVING

SERVES **2**

- 2 skinless, boneless chicken breasts (about 5 ounces each)
- ¼ small napa cabbage, finely shredded
- ½ large carrot, grated
- 1¼ cups bean sprouts
- handful of cilantro, finely chopped
- handful of mint, finely chopped
- ½ red chile, seeded and finely sliced (optional)

Dressing
- 2½ tablespoons sunflower oil
- juice of 1 lime
- ¾ tablespoon Thai fish sauce
- 1½ tablespoons light soy sauce
- ½ tablespoon peeled and finely chopped fresh ginger root

Put the chicken in a bamboo or other steamer set over a large saucepan of boiling water, cover, and cook for about 8 minutes or until the chicken is cooked through. Alternatively, poach the chicken for 8–10 minutes, until cooked and tender.

Meanwhile, make the dressing by combining all the ingredients in a screw-top jar.

When the chicken is cool enough to handle, cut or tear it into strips and mix the pieces with 1 tablespoon of the dressing in a bowl. Let cool.

Toss together all the vegetables, herbs, and chile, if using, in a large bowl, then divide between 2 serving bowls. Spread the cold chicken over the salad and serve immediately with the remaining salad dressing.

Tea-flavored duck with bok choy

PREPARATION TIME **20 MINUTES, PLUS INFUSING** • COOKING TIME **10 MINUTES**

148 CALORIES PER SERVING

SERVES 6

- 3 teaspoons green tea or 3 teabags
- 1 cup boiling water
- 3 duck breasts (about 5 ounces each), with skin
- 3 tablespoons soy sauce
- 4 carrots, cut into matchsticks
- 4 small bok choy, leaves and stems thickly sliced but kept separate
- 3 scallions, sliced
- 2 tablespoons orange liqueur
- juice of 1 orange

Make the tea using a boiling water, let steep for 5 minutes, then strain and cool.

Make crisscross cuts in the duck skin and place the duck, skin side up, in a heatproof shallow glass or ceramic dish. Pour the tea over the duck breasts, cover, and let steep in the refrigerator for 3–4 hours or overnight.

Place the duck breasts in a roasting pan, drizzle 1 tablespoon of the soy sauce over the skin, and roast in a preheated oven, at 425°F, for 10 minutes, until the skin is crispy but the meat is still slightly pink. After 5 minutes, transfer 2 teaspoons of fat from the pan to a skillet or wok.

Reheat the fat, add the carrots, and stir-fry for 2 minutes. Add the bok choy stems and cook for 1 minute. Add the bok choy leaves, scallions, and the remaining soy sauce and cook for 30 seconds. Pour the liqueur over the vegetables, light with a match, and stand well back. When the flames subside, pour in the orange juice and warm through.

Spoon the vegetables into 6 small dishes and top with drained and thinly sliced duck breast. Serve immediately.

Turkey ragout

PREPARATION TIME **10 MINUTES** • COOKING TIME **1 HOUR 50 MINUTES**

190 CALORIES PER SERVING

SERVES 4

- 1 turkey drumstick (about 1¼ pounds)
- 2 garlic cloves
- 15 pearl onions or shallots
- 3 carrots, diagonally sliced
- 1¼ cups red wine
- a few thyme sprigs
- 2 bay leaves
- 2 tablespoons chopped flat-leaf parsley
- 1 teaspoon port wine jelly
- 1 teaspoon whole-grain mustard
- salt and black pepper

Carefully remove the skin from the turkey drumstick and make a few cuts in the flesh. Finely slice 1 of the garlic cloves and push the slivers into the slashes. Crush the remaining garlic clove.

Transfer the drumstick to a large, flameproof casserole or roasting pan with the onions or shallots, carrots, crushed garlic, red wine, thyme, and bay leaves. Season well with salt and black pepper, cover, and place in a preheated oven, at 350°F, for about 1¾ hours or until the turkey is cooked through.

Remove the turkey and vegetables from the casserole and keep hot. Bring the sauce to a boil on the stove, discarding the bay leaves. Add the parsley, port wine jelly, and mustard. Boil for 5 minutes, until slightly thickened. Season with salt and black pepper. Carve the turkey and serve with the juices in 4 serving bowls.

Flounder with coconut crust

PREPARATION TIME **10 MINUTES** • COOKING TIME **15 MINUTES**

195 CALORIES PER SERVING

SERVES **2**

- ¼ cup dried coconut
- ½ cup fresh bread crumbs
- 1 tablespoon chopped chives
- small pinch of paprika
- 2 skinless flounder fillets (about 4 ounces each)
- salt and black pepper
- lime wedges, to serve

Mix together the coconut, bread crumbs, chives, and paprika in a bowl and season with salt and black pepper.

Arrange the fish fillets on a baking sheet and top each one with the coconut mixture.

Place in a preheated oven, at 350°F, for 15 minutes or until cooked through. Serve with lime wedges.

Grilled tuna with shallot jus

PREPARATION TIME **5 MINUTES** • COOKING TIME **15 MINUTES**

240 CALORIES PER SERVING

SERVES **2**

- 2 tuna steaks (about 3½ ounces each)
- flat leaf parsley sprigs, to garnish

Shallot jus
- 2 shallots, finely chopped
- ⅔ cup red wine
- ⅓ cup Marsala wine
- salt and black pepper

Heat a ridged grill pan or a skillet until hot, add the tuna steaks, and cook for 3 minutes on each side. Remove from the pan and keep warm.

To make the shallot jus, mix all the ingredients in a saucepan, season with salt and black pepper, and boil rapidly until the sauce is reduced by half. Return the tuna steaks to the skillet, add the sauce, and simmer for 2 minutes. Serve immediately, garnished with parsley sprigs.

Masala roast cod

150 CALORIES PER SERVING

SERVES 4

- 1 red chile, chopped
- 2 garlic cloves, chopped
- 1 teaspoon peeled and minced fresh ginger root
- 1 teaspoon mustard seeds
- large pinch of ground turmeric
- 2 cloves
- 2 cardamom pods
- 5 peppercorns
- 3 tablespoons water
- 1 teaspoon olive oil
- 3 tablespoons low-fat plain yogurt
- ½ cup fresh bread crumbs
- 1 pound cod fillet
- 2 ripe tomatoes, chopped

To serve
- cilantro leaves
- strips of lemon rind
- lemon and lime wedges

Put the chile, garlic, ginger, mustard seeds, turmeric, cloves, cardamoms, peppercorns, and measured water into a blender or coffee grinder and blend to form a paste. Alternatively, use a mortar and pestle.

Heat the oil in a small saucepan and sauté the chili paste until the oil comes to the surface. Remove the pan from the heat and stir in the yogurt and bread crumbs.

Put the cod into an ovenproof dish and spread the chili paste over it. Spread the tomatoes over the fish, cover with aluminum foil, and put into a preheated oven, at 400°F, for 30 minutes or until the fish is cooked through and tender.

Divide the cod among 4 serving plates, sprinkle with cilantro leaves and strips of lemon rind, and serve with lemon and lime wedges.

Red snapper with baked tomatoes

PREPARATION TIME **20 MINUTES** • COOKING TIME **18–20 MINUTES**

287 CALORIES PER SERVING

SERVES **4**

- 8 red snapper fillets, about 3½ ounces each, scaled and gutted
- finely grated rind of 1 lemon
- 2 teaspoons baby capers, drained
- 2 scallions, finely sliced
- 2½ cups mixed red and yellow cherry tomatoes
- 1½ cups trimmed fine green beans
- 2 garlic cloves, finely chopped
- 1 (2-ounce) can anchovies, drained and chopped
- 1 tablespoon olive oil
- 2 tablespoons lemon juice
- salt and black pepper

To garnish
- 2 tablespoons chopped parsley
- 8 caperberries

Tear off 4 large sheets of aluminum foil and line with nonstick parchment paper. Place 2 fish fillets on each piece of parchment paper, then sprinkle the lemon rind, capers, and scallions over the fish and season with salt and black pepper. Fold over the paper-lined foil and scrunch the edges together to seal. Place the packages on a large baking sheet.

Put the cherry tomatoes in an ovenproof dish with the green beans, garlic, anchovies, oil, and lemon juice. Season with salt and black pepper and mix well.

Bake the vegetables in a preheated oven, at 400°F, for 10 minutes, until tender. Place the fish next to the vegetables in the oven and bake for another 8–10 minutes, until the flesh flakes easily when pressed in the center with a knife.

Spoon the vegetables onto 4 serving plates, then top each with 2 steamed fish fillets. Sprinkle with the chopped parsley, garnish with the caperberries, and serve immediately.

Halibut with papaya salsa

PREPARATION TIME **15 MINUTES** • COOKING TIME **10–12 MINUTES**

236 CALORIES PER SERVING

SERVES **4**

- 2 teaspoons olive oil
- 3 garlic cloves, crushed
- 4 halibut steaks (about 1¼ pounds in total)

Salsa
- 1 papaya, cut into cubes
- ½ red onion, finely chopped
- ⅓ cup finely chopped cilantro leaves
- ¼–½ teaspoon red chili powder
- 1 red bell pepper, cored, seeded, and finely chopped
- juice of ½ lime

To serve
- watercress leaves
- lime wedges

Heat the oil in a large skillet, add the garlic, and stir for a few seconds. Add the fish and cook for 10–12 minutes, until just cooked through, turning halfway through cooking.

Meanwhile, make the salsa by mixing together all the ingredients in a bowl.

Serve the halibut steaks on a bed of watercress leaves, with the salsa and lime wedges.

Aromatic tamarind fish broth

PREPARATION TIME **10 MINUTES** • COOKING TIME **12–15 MINUTES**

123 CALORIES PER SERVING

SERVES **4**

- 20 sprigs cilantro, with roots attached (available in Asian supermarkets)
- 1½-inch cube of peeled fresh ginger root
- 2 tablespoons coarsely chopped onion
- 1 teaspoon shrimp or anchovy paste, or 1 anchovy fillet
- 3 tablespoons water
- 3 cups hot chicken stock
- 1 tablespoon tamarind paste or 2 teaspoons lime juice
- 1 teaspoon packed dark brown sugar
- ¼ teaspoon salt
- 1 pound thick white fish fillets, such as cod, red snapper, or halibut, cut into 4-inch cubes
- 1 scallion, finely sliced

Cut the roots off the cilantro and coarsely chop, then chop the rest of the herb and reserve.

Coarsely chop three-quarters of the ginger and cut the remainder into matchsticks.

Put the cilantro roots, chopped ginger, onion, fish paste or anchovy fillet, and measured water in a blender or food processor and blend to a puree.

Pour the stock into a skillet and add the puree, tamarind paste or lime juice, sugar, and salt and bring to a simmer, then simmer for 5 minutes. Season to taste, if necessary.

Put the fish into the skillet and poach for 1 minute. Gently turn the fish over and cook for another 5–8 minutes, basting frequently, until cooked through.

Transfer the fish to a large serving dish. Pour the poaching liquid over the fish, sprinkle with the scallion, the ginger strips, and the reserved cilantro, and serve.

Broiled sardines with tabbouleh

PREPARATION TIME **15 MINUTES** • COOKING TIME **15 MINUTES**

209 CALORIES PER SERVING

SERVES **4**

- ¾ cup bulgur wheat
- 1 onion, finely chopped
- 2 ripe tomatoes
- 1 tablespoon lemon juice
- 1 teaspoon grated lemon rind
- small handful of mint leaves
- 4 small sardines, gutted and boned
- salt and black pepper

To serve
- lemon wedges
- salad greens

Cook the bulgur wheat in a small saucepan of boiling water for 5 minutes, then drain and refresh under cold running water. Drain again and put into a bowl.

Meanwhile, dry-fry the onion in a small, nonstick skillet for 5 minutes. Put the tomatoes in a large saucepan or heatproof bowl and pour over enough boiling water to cover, then let stand for about 1 minute. Drain, skin the tomatoes carefully, then seed and finely chop the flesh.

Add the onion, tomatoes, and lemon juice and rind to the bulgur wheat. Reserve 4 mint leaves, then chop the remainder. Stir the chopped mint into the bulgur wheat mixture and season with salt and black pepper.

Open out each sardine and lay a mint leaf along the center. Spoon over a little of the tabbouleh and carefully fold the fillet back over. Cook the sardines under a preheated broiler for 5 minutes, then carefully turn them over and cook for another 5 minutes or until cooked through. Serve with the remaining tabbouleh (hot or cold), lemon wedges, and a few salad greens.

Sesame-crusted salmon

PREPARATION TIME **10 MINUTES** • COOKING TIME **9–12 MINUTES**

324 CALORIES PER SERVING

SERVES 2

- 2 tablespoons sesame seeds
- ½ teaspoon dried red pepper flakes
- 2 salmon fillets (about 3½ ounces each)
- 1 teaspoon olive oil
- 1 carrot, cut into matchsticks
- 1 red bell pepper, cored, seeded, and thinly sliced
- 3½ ounces shiitake mushrooms, halved
- 1 bok choy, quartered lengthwise
- 2 scallions, shredded
- ½ tablespoon soy sauce

Mix together the sesame seeds and red pepper flakes on a plate, then press the salmon fillets into the mixture until covered.

Heat half the oil in a skillet or wok, add the salmon, and cook over medium heat for 3–4 minutes on each side, until cooked through. Remove from the skillet and keep warm.

Heat the remaining oil in the skillet, add the vegetables, and stir-fry for 3–4 minutes, until just cooked. Drizzle the soy sauce over the vegetables, then serve with the salmon.

Chile & cilantro fish package

PREPARATION TIME **15 MINUTES, PLUS MARINATING AND CHILLING** • COOKING TIME **15 MINUTES**

127 CALORIES PER SERVING

SERVES 1

- **4 ounces cod, coley, or halibut fillet**
- **2 teaspoons lemon juice**
- **1 tablespoon cilantro leaves, plus extra to garnish**
- **1 garlic clove**
- **1 green chile, seeded and chopped, plus extra to garnish**
- **¼ teaspoon sugar**
- **2 teaspoons plain yogurt**

Put the fish into a nonmetallic dish and sprinkle with the lemon juice. Cover and let marinate in the refrigerator for 15–20 minutes.

Put the cilantro, garlic, and chile in a mini food processor and blend until the mixture forms a paste. Add the sugar and yogurt and briefly process to blend.

Lay the fish on a sheet of parchment paper or aluminum foil and coat on both sides with the paste. Gather up the parchment or foil loosely around the fish and turn over at the top to seal. Chill for at least 1 hour.

Place the package on a baking sheet and bake in a preheated oven, at 400°F, for about 15 minutes or until the fish is just cooked through. Serve garnished with extra chile and cilantro.

Fish & tomato curry

194 CALORIES PER SERVING

SERVES **4**

- 2 tablespoons vegetable oil
- 1 onion, finely chopped
- 4 garlic cloves, sliced
- 1 teaspoon peeled and grated fresh ginger root
- ½ teaspoon ground turmeric
- 1 teaspoon chili powder
- 1 teaspoon ground cumin
- 2 teaspoons ground coriander
- 1 teaspoon garam masala
- 1 pound thick white fish fillets, such as cod or halibut, cut into 1-inch cubes
- 1⅔ cups canned diced tomatoes
- 2 teaspoons sea salt
- 2 teaspoons sugar

Heat the oil in a large skillet, add the onion, and sauté until soft and lightly browned. Add the garlic, ginger, and spices and sauté for 30 seconds. Add the fish and stir gently for another 1 minute.

Add the tomatoes, salt, and sugar and stir gently. Cover and simmer gently for 7–10 minutes or until the fish is cooked through. Serve hot.

TOP TIP

It takes 20 minutes for your brain to register that your stomach is full, so eating slowly is a great way to stop you from overeating on your "off" days.

Squid, chickpea & vegetable stew

PREPARATION TIME **10 MINUTES** • COOKING TIME **25 MINUTES**

331 CALORIES PER SERVING

SERVES **1**

- 1 tablespoon all-purpose flour
- 13 ounces prepared squid rings
- 2 tablespoons olive oil
- 1 fennel bulb, trimmed and chopped
- 2 green bell peppers, cored, seeded, and sliced
- 2 garlic cloves, crushed
- 1 tablespoon chopped oregano
- 2½ cups fish stock
- 2½ cups rinsed and drained canned chickpeas
- squeeze of lemon juice
- 8 cherry tomatoes, halved
- salt and black pepper

Season the flour and use it to dust the squid rings. Heat the oil in a large saucepan, add the fennel and bell peppers, and sauté gently for 5 minutes. Add the garlic and oregano and sauté for another 5 minutes.

Add the squid and continue to cook for 5 minutes or until puffed into rings. Stir in the stock and chickpeas and bring to a simmer. Cook gently, covered, for 10 minutes.

Add the lemon juice and tomatoes and season with salt and black pepper. Cook for another 1 minute, then serve.

Lemony scallop skewers

238 CALORIES PER SERVING

SERVES 2

- 6 ounces scallops, without roes
- finely grated rind of ½ lemon
- 1½ teaspoons basil oil
- 3 tablespoons hazelnuts, blanched
- 3½ cups arugula
- ½ tablespoon lemon juice
- salt and black pepper

Put the scallops in a bowl with the lemon rind and 1 teaspoon of the basil oil and season with black pepper. Mix well to coat.

Thread the scallops onto 2 metal skewers and cook under a preheated broiler for 2–3 minutes, turning occasionally, until just cooked through, firm, and opaque.

Meanwhile, heat a small skillet over medium heat, then add the hazelnuts and dry-fry until golden brown, shaking the pan frequently. Transfer the nuts to a small dish and crush lightly.

Toss the arugula with the remaining basil oil, the lemon juice, and salt and black pepper. Arrange on 2 serving plates and top each with a scallop skewer. Sprinkle the hazelnuts over the top and serve immediately.

Aromatic steamed mussels

PREPARATION TIME **20 MINUTES** • COOKING TIME **15–17 MINUTES**

185 CALORIES PER SERVING

SERVES **2**

- 1½ pounds fresh mussels, soaked in cold water
- ½ tablespoon peanut oil
- 1 shallot, thinly sliced
- ½ red chile, seeded and finely sliced
- ½-inch piece of fresh ginger root, peeled and finely chopped
- ½ garlic clove, finely sliced
- 1½ tablespoons licorice-flavored liqueur, such as Pernod
- ¾ cup fish or vegetable stock
- ½ small preserved lemon, finely chopped
- ½ small bunch of cilantro, coarsely chopped
- salt and black pepper

Discard any mussels that are open or have cracked shells. Scrub with a small nail brush, remove any barnacles, and pull off any small, hairy beards. Return the mussels to a bowl of clean, cold water.

Heat the oil in a large, heavy casserole over medium-low heat, then stir in the shallot, chile, ginger, and garlic and cook gently for 7–8 minutes or until softened, stirring occasionally. Add the alcohol and simmer until evaporated, then add the stock and preserved lemon and bring to a boil.

Drain the mussels and transfer to the pan. Season with salt and black pepper, then stir the mussels to coat them in the shallot mixture. Cover with a tight-fitting lid and steam gently, shaking the pan occasionally, for 4–5 minutes. Halfway through cooking, use a large metal spoon to stir the mussels thoroughly, lifting the ones from the bottom of the pan to the top. Replace the lid and cook until the mussels have opened.

Heap the mussels into 2 deep serving bowls, discarding any shells that have not opened. Sprinkle with the cilantro and serve immediately with a large bowl to the side for the empty shells.

Clams with chorizo & pimentón

PREPARATION TIME **25 MINUTES** • COOKING TIME **15–17 MINUTES**

257 CALORIES PER SERVING

SERVES 4

- 3 pounds fresh clams, soaked in cold water
- 6 tomatoes
- 2 tablespoons olive oil
- 1 large onion, finely chopped
- 2–3 garlic cloves, finely chopped
- ¼ teaspoon ground pimentón (smoked paprika)
- 1¾ cups fish stock
- 3 ounces sliced chorizo sausage, diced
- salt and black pepper
- chopped parsley, to garnish

Discard any clams that are open or have cracked shells. Scrub with a small nail brush, remove any barnacles, and pull off any small, hairy beards. Return the clams to a bowl of clean, cold water.

Put the tomatoes in a large saucepan or heatproof bowl and pour over enough boiling water to cover, then let stand for about 1 minute. Drain, skin the tomatoes carefully, and then seed and dice the flesh.

Heat the oil in a large saucepan, add the onion, and sauté for 5 minutes, until softened and lightly browned. Stir in the garlic and pimentón and cook for another 1 minute. Stir in the tomatoes, stock, and chorizo, season with salt and black pepper, and simmer for 3–4 minutes.

Drain the clams and transfer them to the pan, cover with a tight-fitting lid, and cook for 5–7 minutes, until the clams have opened. Spoon the clams and the sauce into 4 shallow serving bowls, discarding any shells that have not opened. Garnish with parsley and serve immediately.

Seafood zarzuela

PREPARATION TIME **30 MINUTES** • COOKING TIME **25 MINUTES**

240 CALORIES PER SERVING

SERVES 4

- 4 tomatoes
- 1 tablespoon olive oil
- 1 large onion, finely chopped
- 2 garlic cloves, finely chopped
- ½ teaspoon pimentón (smoked paprika)
- 1 red bell pepper, cored, seeded, and diced
- 1 cup fish stock
- ⅔ cup dry white wine
- 2 large pinches of saffron threads
- 4 small bay leaves
- 1 pound fresh mussels, soaked in cold water
- 7 ounces squid, cleaned and rinsed in cold water
- 12 ounces skinless cod loin, cubed
- salt and black pepper

Put the tomatoes in a large saucepan or heatproof bowl and pour over enough boiling water to cover, then let stand for about 1 minute. Drain, skin the tomatoes carefully, and then coarsely chop the flesh.

Heat the oil in a large saucepan, add the onion, and sauté for 5 minutes, until softened and just beginning to brown. Stir in the garlic and pimentón and cook for another 1 minute.

Stir in the tomatoes, red bell pepper, stock, wine, and saffron. Add the bay leaves, season with salt and black pepper, and bring to a boil. Cover and simmer gently for 10 minutes, then remove the pan from the heat and set aside.

Discard any mussels that are open or have cracked shells. Scrub with a small nail brush, remove any barnacles, and pull off any small, hairy beards. Return the mussels to a bowl of clean water. Separate the squid tubes from the tentacles, then slice the tubes.

Reheat the tomato sauce, if necessary, add the cod and sliced squid, and cook for 2 minutes. Drain the mussels and transfer to the pan, cover with a tight-fitting lid, and cook for 4 minutes. Add the squid tentacles and cook for another 2 minutes, until the fish is cooked through and all the mussels have opened. Gently stir, then serve, discarding any mussels that have not opened.

Green peppercorn steak

130
CALORIES
PER SERVING

SERVES
2

- 2 lean tenderloin steaks (about 3 ounces each)
- ½ tablespoon green peppercorns in brine, drained
- 1 tablespoon light soy sauce
- ½ teaspoon balsamic vinegar
- 4 cherry tomatoes, halved
- thyme sprigs, to garnish

Heat a ridged grill pan or skillet until hot, add the steaks, and cook for 2–3 minutes on each side, then remove from the pan and keep warm.

Add the peppercorns, soy sauce, vinegar, and tomatoes to the pan. Let the liquids sizzle for 2 minutes or until the tomatoes are soft. Spoon the sauce over the steaks and serve garnished with thyme sprigs.

Thai beef & bell pepper stir-fry

255
CALORIES
PER SERVING

SERVES
4

- 1 pound lean tenderloin steak
- 1 tablespoon sesame oil
- 1 garlic clove, finely chopped
- 1 lemon grass stalk, finely shredded
- 1-inch piece of fresh ginger root, peeled and finely chopped
- 1 red bell pepper, cored, seeded, and thickly sliced
- 1 green bell pepper, cored, seeded, and thickly sliced
- 1 onion, thickly sliced
- 2 tablespoons lime juice
- black pepper

Cut the beef into long, thin strips, cutting across the grain. Heat the oil in a wok or large skillet over high heat, add the garlic, and stir-fry for 1 minute. Add the steak and stir-fry for 2–3 minutes, until lightly brown. Stir in the lemon grass and ginger and remove the pan from the heat. Remove the steak from the pan and set aside.

Add the bell peppers and onion to the pan and stir-fry for 2–3 minutes, until the onions are just turning golden brown and are slightly softened. Return the steak to the pan, stir in the lime juice, and season with black pepper.

Russian meatballs

154 CALORIES PER SERVING

SERVES 4

- 12 ounces low-fat ground beef
- 1 onion, coarsely chopped
- 1 tablespoon tomato paste
- 1 teaspoon dried mixed herbs
- salt and black pepper
- chopped parsley and parsley sprigs, to garnish
- mashed potatoes, to serve (optional)

Tomato sauce
- 1 red onion, finely chopped
- 1⅔ cups canned diced tomatoes
- pinch of paprika, plus extra to garnish
- 1 teaspoon dried mixed herbs

Put the beef, onion, tomato paste, and dried mixed herbs in a blender or food processor. Season well with salt and black pepper and blend until smooth. Shape the mixture into 12 balls and chill for 30 minutes.

Meanwhile, put all the tomato sauce ingredients in a saucepan and cook, uncovered, over low heat for 15–20 minutes, stirring occasionally.

Season the sauce with salt and black pepper and transfer to an ovenproof dish. Arrange the meatballs on top and put into a preheated oven, at 350°F, for 45 minutes. Sprinkle the meatballs with chopped parsley and paprika and garnished with parsley sprigs. Serve with mashed potatoes, if desired (remembering to count the calories).

Lean lasagna

340 CALORIES PER SERVING

SERVES **8**

- **7 ounces ready-to-bake lasagna noodles**
- **black pepper**

Meat sauce
- **2 eggplants, peeled and diced**
- **2 red onions, chopped**
- **2 garlic cloves, crushed**
- **1¼ cups vegetable stock**
- **¼ cup red wine**
- **1 pound ground round beef**
- **3⅓ cups cans diced tomatoes**

Cheese sauce
- **3 egg whites**
- **1 cup ricotta cheese**
- **¾ cup milk**
- **¼cup plus 2 tablespoons grated Parmesan cheese**

To make the meat sauce, put the eggplants, onions, garlic, stock, and wine in a large saucepan. Cover and simmer briskly for 5 minutes.

Remove the lid and cook for about another 5 minutes, until the eggplant is tender and the liquid is absorbed, adding a little more stock, if necessary. Remove from the heat and let cool slightly, then puree in a blender or food processor.

Meanwhile, brown the beef in a nonstick skillet. Skim off any fat. Add the eggplant mixture and tomatoes and season with black pepper. Simmer briskly, uncovered, for about 10 minutes, until thickened.

To make the cheese sauce, beat the egg whites with the ricotta in a bowl, then beat in the milk and ¼ cup of the Parmesan. Season with black pepper.

Alternate layers of the meat sauce, lasagna noodles, and cheese sauce in an ovenproof dish, starting with the meat sauce and finishing with the cheese sauce. Sprinkle the top with the remaining Parmesan. Bake in a preheated oven, at 350°F, for 30–40 minutes, until browned. Serve hot.

Lemon & caper pork tenderloin

PREPARATION TIME **20 MINUTES** • COOKING TIME **16–17 MINUTES**

320 CALORIES PER SERVING

SERVES 4

- **2 thin pork tenderloins (about 10 ounces each), cut in half**
- **1 garlic clove, coarsely chopped**
- **1 tablespoon chopped sage**
- **finely grated rind and juice of 1 lemon**
- **4 teaspoons olive oil**
- **2 teaspoons honey**
- **1 tablespoon capers, drained**
- **2 long banana shallots, chopped**
- **5½ cups coarsely sliced baby leaf spinach**
- **salt and black pepper**
- **8–12 caperberries, to garnish**

Slice the pork horizontally without cutting all the way through and open up each piece like a butterfly. Place the garlic, sage, lemon rind, 2 teaspoons of the oil, honey, capers, and 1 teaspoon of the lemon juice in a mini food processor and blend to a coarse paste. Rub the mixture all over the pork.

Heat a large nonstick skillet over medium heat, add the pork, and sauté for 1 minute to seal, turning once. Transfer the meat to a small roasting pan, season with salt and black pepper, and roast in a preheated oven, at 425°F, for 10 minutes or until cooked through and the juices run clear. Remove from the oven, cover with aluminum foil, and let rest.

Meanwhile, heat the remaining oil in a skillet over low heat, add the shallots, and cook for 5–6 minutes, until softened. Add the spinach leaves to the skillet and stir until wilted. Stir in the remaining lemon juice, season with salt and black pepper, then spoon onto 4 serving plates. Place the pork on top and serve scattered with caperberries.

Pork skewers with coleslaw

PREPARATION TIME **25 MINUTES, PLUS MARINATING** • COOKING TIME **7–10 MINUTES**

296 CALORIES PER SERVING

SERVES 4

- 1¼ pounds lean pork loin, cubed

Barbecue marinade
- 2 tablespoons packed light brown sugar
- 2 tablespoons ketchup
- 2 tablespoons dark soy sauce
- 1 teaspoon Chinese 5-spice powder
- 2 tablespoons orange juice

Coleslaw
- 1 tablespoon red wine vinegar
- 2 teaspoons piri-piri sauce or marinade
- ½ teaspoon granulated sugar
- ¼–⅓ cup extra-light mayonnaise
- ½ red cabbage, shredded
- 2 carrots, grated
- 2 scallions, thinly sliced
- salt and black pepper

Mix together the marinade ingredients in a large nonmetallic bowl until smooth. Add the pork and mix until well coated. Let marinate for 15 minutes.

Meanwhile, make the coleslaw. Mix together the vinegar, piri-piri sauce, sugar, and mayonnaise in a small bowl. Toss the cabbage, carrots, and scallions together in a large bowl, then add the dressing and mix together until well combined. Season with salt and black pepper and set aside.

Thread the pork onto 8 metal skewers and cook under a preheated broiler for 7–10 minutes, turning occasionally, until cooked through and sticky. Serve 2 skewers per person with the coleslaw.

Herbed lamb with lima beans

PREPARATION TIME **15 MINUTES, PLUS CHILLING** • COOKING TIME **10 MINUTES**

305 CALORIES PER SERVING

SERVES **4**

- 2 tablespoons finely chopped mint
- 1 tablespoon finely chopped thyme
- 1 tablespoon finely chopped oregano
- ½ tablespoon finely chopped rosemary
- 4 teaspoons whole-grain mustard
- 4 boned and rolled lamb loin chops (noisettes, about 4 ounces each)

Tangy lima beans
- 2 teaspoons sunflower oil
- 1 onion, chopped
- 1 cup cooked lima beans or drained canned lima beans
- 1 tablespoon tomato paste
- ¼ cup pineapple juice
- 2 tablespoons lemon juice
- a few drops of Tabasco sauce
- black pepper

Mix together all the chopped herbs in a bowl. Spread mustard on both sides of each lamb chop and dip the meat into the herb mixture. Press the herbs firmly to the mustard. Chill the lamb until you are ready to cook.

To make the tangy lima beans, heat the oil in a skillet, add the onion, and sauté until softened. Add the remaining ingredients and cook gently for 5 minutes.

Meanwhile, cook the lamb chops under a preheated hot broiler for about 4 minutes on each side, until cooked but still slightly pink in the center. Serve immediately with the lima beans.

TOP TIP

Plan your fasting days at the beginning of the week. It is a good idea to fast on days when you will be busy because you won't have so much time to think about food if you have a long list of things to do.

Lamb & bean stew

PREPARATION TIME **10 MINUTES** • COOKING TIME **1 HOUR 20 MINUTES**

288 CALORIES PER SERVING

SERVES 4

- 1 teaspoon olive oil
- 11½ ounces lean lamb, cubed
- 16 pearl onions, peeled
- 1 garlic clove, crushed
- 1 tablespoon all-purpose flour
- 2½ cups lamb stock
- ¾ canned diced tomatoes
- 1 bouquet garni
- 3 cups rinsed and drained canned great Northern beans
- 16 cherry tomatoes
- black pepper

Heat the oil in a flameproof casserole or saucepan, add the lamb, and cook for 3–4 minutes, until browned all over. Remove from the casserole and set aside.

Add the onions and garlic to the skillet and sauté for 4–5 minutes, until the onions are beginning to brown.

Return the lamb and any juices to the skillet, then stir through the flour and add the stock, canned tomatoes, bouquet garni, and beans. Bring to a boil, stirring, then cover and simmer for 1 hour, until the lamb is just tender.

Add the cherry tomatoes to the skillet, season well with black pepper, and simmer for another 10 minutes, then serve hot.

TOP TIP

Try drinking green tea. It contains no calories, is rich in antioxidants, and may even marginally increase your metabolic rate, giving you a slight weight-loss advantage.

Turkish lamb & potato stew

PREPARATION TIME **20 MINUTES** • COOKING TIME **2–2¼ HOURS**

307 CALORIES PER SERVING

SERVES **6**

- 3 tomatoes
- 1 tablespoon vegetable oil
- 1 pound lean lamb, cut into ¾-inch cubes
- 4 onions, cut into wedges
- 2 garlic cloves, crushed
- 6 Yukon gold or red-skinned potatoes, peeled and cut into chunks
- 1 red or green bell pepper, cored, seeded, and sliced
- 3¾ cups stock or water
- 2 tablespoons wine vinegar
- 2 bay leaves
- 1 teaspoon chopped sage
- 1 tablespoon chopped dill or fennel leaves
- 1 eggplant and/or 1 trimmed and chopped fennel bulb
- 12 pitted ripe black olives
- black pepper

Put the tomatoes in a large saucepan or heatproof bowl and pour over enough boiling water to cover, then let stand for about 1 minute. Drain, skin the tomatoes carefully, and then quarter or slice the flesh.

Heat the oil in a large, heavy saucepan, add the lamb, and cook, stirring, until sealed and browned all over.

Add the onions and garlic and sauté gently for about 5 minutes, until softened. Add the potatoes, tomatoes, bell pepper, stock or water, and vinegar and bring to a boil. Add the herbs and season well with black pepper. Cover and simmer gently for 1 hour.

Stir well, then add the eggplant and/or fennel and olives. Bring back to a boil, cover, and simmer gently for 45–60 minutes, until the lamb is tender, stirring occasionally. Discard the bay leaves before serving.

Veal with lemon

PREPARATION TIME **10 MINUTES** • COOKING TIME **40–45 MINUTES**

368 CALORIES PER SERVING

SERVES **4**

- 2 tablespoons olive oil
- 2 pounds veal, cubed
- 2 onions, sliced
- 4 garlic cloves, sliced
- 2 baby fennel bulbs, trimmed and coarsely chopped
- 2 cups white wine
- 2 cups chicken stock
- rind of ½ lemon, cut into matchsticks
- 4 bay leaves
- 1 tablespoon thyme leaves
- salt and black pepper

Heat the oil in a large skillet over high heat, add the veal, and brown evenly. Remove from the skillet with a slotted spoon and set aside.

Add the onion and garlic to the skillet and sauté over medium heat until golden brown. Add the fennel and sauté for another 3-4 minutes or until softened.

Return the veal to the skillet and add the wine, stock, lemon rind, bay leaves, and thyme. Bring to a boil and boil for 5 minutes. Reduce the heat, cover, and simmer for another 20–25 minutes. Season and serve hot.

TOP TIP

Reward yourself for your successes. Set yourself targets and, once you have reached them, treat yourself to something nice.

Liver with garlic mashed potatoes

PREPARATION TIME **10 MINUTES** • COOKING TIME **12–16 MINUTES**

393 CALORIES PER SERVING

SERVES 2

- 3 russet or Yukon gold potatoes, peeled and cubed
- 1 garlic clove
- 3 tablespoons light crème fraîche or Greek yogurt
- ½ tablespoon chopped sage
- 2 slices of liver (about 5 ounces each)
- 1 tablespoon seasoned flour
- ½ tablespoon olive oil
- salt and black pepper
- gravy, to serve

Cook the potatoes and garlic in a saucepan of lightly salted boiling water for 10–12 minutes, until tender, then drain. Return the potatoes and garlic to the pan and mash with the crème fraîche or yogurt and sage. Season well with black pepper.

Meanwhile, press the pieces of liver into the seasoned flour to coat them all over. Heat the oil in a skillet, add the liver, and cook for 1–2 minutes on each side or until cooked to your liking. Serve with the mashed potatoes and gravy.

Orangey baked nectarines

PREPARATION TIME **5 MINUTES** • COOKING TIME **18–20 MINUTES**

161 CALORIES PER SERVING • SERVES **2**

- 2 tablespoons orange liqueur, such as Cointreau
- ½ teaspoon vanilla extract
- finely grated rind of ¼ orange
- 1 tablespoon honey
- 2 firm, ripe nectarines, halved and pitted
- ⅓ cup nonfat Greek yogurt with honey, to serve

Put the orange liqueur, vanilla extract, orange rind, and honey in a bowl and stir until well combined.

Arrange the nectarines, cut side up, in an ovenproof dish, then drizzle with the liqueur mixture. Bake in a preheated oven, at 350°F, for 18–20 minutes ,until tender.

Divide the nectarines between 2 serving bowls and serve with the yogurt, drizzled with any juices from the pan.

Creole pineapple wedges

PREPARATION TIME **10 MINUTES** • COOKING TIME **8–10 MINUTES**

159 CALORIES PER SERVING

SERVES 4

- 1 small pineapple (about 2½ pounds)
- 1 tablespoon dark rum
- juice of 1 lime
- 1½ tablespoons sesame seeds

Cut the pineapple lengthwise, first in half and then into quarters, leaving the leaves intact. The wedges should be about ½ inch thick, so it may be necessary to divide the quarters again.

Mix together the dark rum and lime juice in a bowl and sprinkle the mixture over the pineapple slices.

Toast the pineapple under a preheated hot broiler for 8–10 minutes, turning to make sure of even cooking. Serve immediately, sprinkled with the sesame seeds.

Bananas en papillote

PREPARATION TIME **5 MINUTES** • COOKING TIME **3–4 MINUTES**

95
CALORIES
PER SERVING

SERVES
4

- butter, for greasing
- 4 small, firm bananas
- 1 cinnamon stick, cut into 4
- 4 star anise
- 1 vanilla bean, cut into 4
- 2 tablespoons grated semisweet chocolate
- ⅓ cup pineapple juice

Lightly grease 4 pieces of aluminum foil or nonstick parchment paper, each large enough to wrap a banana.

Place a banana in the center of each piece and add a piece of cinnamon stick, 1 star anise, and a piece of vanilla bean to each. Sprinkle with the grated chocolate and pineapple juice. Fold up the packages and seal to make airtight pockets.

Place the packages on a baking sheet and bake in a preheated oven, at 450°F, for 3–4 minutes. Alternatively, cook on top of a barbecue; in this case, use a double-thickness of foil to prevent splits and spillages. Serve warm.

Peach consommé with raspberries

PREPARATION TIME **10 MINUTES, PLUS CHILLING** • COOKING TIME **20 MINUTES**

124 CALORIES PER SERVING

SERVES **4**

• 2½ cups water
• 1 vanilla bean
• 1 star anise
• 1 cinnamon stick
• 3 tablespoons honey
• 8 peaches
• juice of 1 lemon

To decorate
• 1 cup raspberries
• mint sprigs

Put the measured water, vanilla bean, star anise, cinnamon stick, and honey in a large saucepan. Bring to a boil and simmer for 5 minutes. Add the peaches and poach for 5 minutes, then remove 4 of them with a slotted spoon and let cool.

Add the lemon juice to the reserved liquid and simmer the remaining peaches for another 10 minutes, until mushy.

Meanwhile, gently peel the skins away from the cooled peaches and chill in the refrigerator.

Remove the pits from the mushy peaches and blend the pulp and cooking liquid in a blender or food processor. Push the puree through a fine strainer and chill.

When ready to serve, place 1 poached peach in each of 4 serving bowls and pour one-quarter of the fruit consommé over the top of each. Decorate with the raspberries and sprigs of mint and serve.

Apple & berry strudels

PREPARATION TIME **7 MINUTES** • COOKING TIME **20 MINUTES**

- 2 cooking apples, such as Granny Smiths or Pippins, peeled and grated
- 1½ cups mixed berries
- pinch of ground cinnamon
- 1 tablespoon honey
- 2 sheets of phyllo pastry
- 1 egg white
- mint sprigs, to decorate
- low-fat custard or whipped cream, to serve (optional)

Put the grated apples, berries, cinnamon, and 1 teaspoon of the honey in a saucepan and cook gently for about 5 minutes or until the fruit is soft.

Brush the phyllo sheets with egg white and place 1 sheet on top of the other. Cut the sheets into quarters and place one-quarter of the fruit in the center of each rectangle. Tuck in the ends of the pastry and roll into log shapes.

Place the strudels on a baking sheet, brush with the remaining honey, and bake in a preheated oven, at 300°F, for 15 minutes or until golden brown.

Decorate the strudels with sprigs of mint and serve with a little low-fat custard or whipped cream, if desired (remembering to count the calories).

Chinese spiced citrus salad

PREPARATION TIME **15 MINUTES, PLUS INFUSING AND CHILLING** • COOKING TIME **5 MINUTES**

163 CALORIES PER SERVING

SERVES 4

- 3 oranges, peeled and pith removed, separated into segments
- 1 ruby grapefruit, peeled and pith removed, separated into segments
- 1 banana, thinly sliced
- ⅔ cup low-fat crème fraîche or Greek yogurt, to serve

Syrup
- 1 whole clove
- ¼ teaspoon Chinese 5-spice powder
- rind of 1 lime
- 1 vanilla bean, split lengthwise
- ¼ teaspoon peeled and grated fresh ginger root
- 1¼ cups water

To decorate
- 1 tablespoon finely chopped mint
- seeds of 1 pomegranate

To make the syrup, combine all the ingredients in a saucepan, bring to a boil, and simmer gently for 3–5 minutes. Remove the pan from the heat and let the syrup steep and cool.

Meanwhile, mix together the orange and grapefruit segments in an attractive glass serving bowl. Add the banana slices.

Pour the cooled syrup through a strainer to remove the solids, then pour it over the fruits. Cover and chill for 2–3 hours.

Divide the fruit salad among 4 serving bowls, top with the crème fraîche or yogurt, and serve decorated with the mint and pomegranate seeds.

TOP TIP

The average food craving lasts about 10 minutes, so try to distract yourself to get past your hunger pang. Make yourself a cup of herbal tea, have a bath, or phone a friend.

Honeyed figs

- 8 fresh figs, halved
- 1 tablespoon honey
- 3 ounces goat cheese, cut into 4 thin slices
- 1 cup raspberries
- handful of flat-leaf parsley, chopped, to decorate

Put the figs, cut side up, in an aluminum foil-lined broiler pan and drizzle a little honey into the center of each. Cook under a preheated hot broiler for 2–3 minutes.

Transfer to 4 serving plates and serve hot with the goat cheese and raspberries, sprinkled with the parsley.

Mango & passion fruit trifle

- 2 ladyfingers
- ⅓ cup nonfat Greek yogurt
- ½ cup low-fat crème fraîche or extra Greek yogurt
- 2 passion fruit
- ½ mango, peeled, pitted, and diced

Break each ladyfinger into 4 pieces and divide among 2 glasses. Mix together the yogurt and crème fraîche in a bowl.

Halve the passion fruit and remove the seeds. Spoon the seeds over the fingers, then add half of the mango pieces.

Pour half the crème fraîche mixture over the fruit, then top with the remaining mango. Spoon over the remaining crème fraîche and top with the remaining passion fruit. Chill for 1 hour before serving.

Mango & clementine sorbet

PREPARATION TIME 20 MINUTES, PLUS COOLING AND FREEZING • COOKING TIME 5 MINUTES

95 CALORIES PER SERVING

SERVES **6**

- 1 cup water
- ¼ cup firmly packed light brown sugar
- 7 clementines, halved
- 2 large mangoes, pitted and peeled
- 1 egg white
- grated rind and juice of 1 lime

Put the measured water in a small saucepan and add the sugar. Gently bring to a boil and heat until the sugar has dissolved. Remove the pan from the heat and let the syrup cool.

Squeeze the juice from the clementines. Puree the flesh of 1 of the mangoes until it is smooth. Stir the mango puree and clementine juice into the cooled sugar syrup and mix together.

Pour the mixture into a plastic container, cover, and freeze for 2–3 hours, until semifrozen. Beat well with a fork or blend in a food processor to break up the ice crystals, then repeat the freezing and beating process. Mix in the egg white, then freeze until solid.

Alternatively, churn the mixture in an ice cream maker for 20–30 minutes, until the sorbet is thick. Add the egg white and continue churning until the sorbet is well mixed and thick enough to scoop. Serve immediately or transfer to a plastic container and store in the freezer until required.

Take the sorbet out of the freezer and let soften at room temperature for 15 minutes before serving. Slice the remaining mango and toss the slices in the lime juice and rind mixture. Scoop the sorbet into 6 serving dishes and serve with the mango slices.

Champagne granita

80 CALORIES PER SERVING

SERVES **6**

- ⅔ cup water
- 3 tablespoons light brown sugar
- 1½ cups medium-dry champagne
- 1 cup wild or small strawberries

Put the measured water in a small saucepan and add the sugar. Gently bring to a boil and heat until the sugar has dissolved. Remove the pan from the heat and let the syrup cool.

Mix together the cooled sugar syrup and champagne, then pour the mixture into a shallow, nonstick baking pan so that it is no more than 1 inch deep.

Freeze the mixture for 2 hours, until it is mushy, then break up the ice crystals with a fork. Return the mixture to the freezer for another 2 hours, beating every 30 minutes, until it has formed fine, icy flakes.

To serve, spoon the granita and the strawberries into 6 dessert glasses and serve immediately.

Coconut & lime ice cream

PREPARATION TIME **20 MINUTES, PLUS COOLING AND FREEZING** • COOKING TIME **5 MINUTES**

168 CALORIES PER SERVING

SERVES **4**

- ⅔ cup water
- ⅓ cup firmly packed light brown sugar
- 6 dried kaffir lime leaves
- finely grated rind of 1 lemon
- 1⅔ cups reduced-fat coconut milk
- lemon or lime rind curls, to decorate

Put the measured water into a small saucepan and add the sugar. Gently bring to a boil and heat until the sugar has dissolved. Remove the pan from the heat and add the lime leaves, then cover and let the syrup cool and steep for at least 2 hours.

Remove the lime leaves from the cooled syrup and reserve. Mix the syrup with the lemon rind and coconut milk.

Pour the mixture into a plastic container, cover, and freeze for 6–8 hours, beating 2 or 3 times with a fork to break up the ice crystals.

Alternatively, churn the mixture in an ice cream maker for 20–30 minutes, until thick and spoonable. Serve immediately, or transfer to a plastic container and store in the freezer until required.

Take the ice cream out of the freezer and let soften at room temperature for 15 minutes before serving. Scoop the ice cream into 4 small glasses and serve decorated with the reserved lime leaves.

Chocolate orange soufflés

178 CALORIES PER SERVING

SERVES 6

- ⅓ cup orange juice
- ⅓ cup superfine sugar (or granulated sugar blended in a food processor for 1 minute)
- 4 extra-large egg whites
- ¼ cup unsweetened cocoa powder
- 2 tablespoons orange liqueur
- vegetable oil, for greasing
- 1 cup low-fat vanilla ice cream, softened

Put the orange juice and sugar in a small saucepan and heat for 3–4 minutes over medium-high heat, stirring occasionally until the mixture has a syrupy consistency. Remove the pan from the heat.

In a large, clean bowl, whisk the egg whites until stiff, but stop before dry peaks form. Pour the syrup over the egg whites and beat for 2 minutes. Add the cocoa powder and liqueur and beat briefly until well mixed.

Pour the batter into 6 lightly greased ovenproof cups and bake in a preheated oven, at 425°F, for 8–10 minutes or until the soufflés are puffed. Do not overcook or the soufflés will become tough.

Spoon 2 tablespoons of the softened ice cream into the center of each soufflé and serve immediately.

Pimm's gelatins

85 CALORIES PER SERVING

SERVES **6**

- 3 tablespoons water
- 3 teaspoons powdered gelatin
- 1 crisp sweet apple, such as Pippin, cored and diced
- 1 tablespoon lemon juice
- 1½ cups hulled and sliced strawberries
- 1 peach, halved, pitted, and diced
- 1 orange, peeled and cut into segments
- ⅔ cup Pimm's No. 1
- 2 cups diet lemon-flavored soda, chilled

To decorate
- peach slices
- strawberries, hulled and halved
- mint sprigs or borage flowers
- orange rind curls

Put the measured water in a small, heatproof bowl and sprinkle the gelatin over the top, making sure that all the powder is absorbed by the water. Let soak for 5 minutes. Stand the bowl in a small saucepan of gently simmering water so that the water comes halfway up the sides of the bowl. Heat for 4–5 minutes, until the gelatin has dissolved and the liquid is clear.

Meanwhile, put the apple pieces in a bowl and toss with the lemon juice. Add the other fruits, mix together, and divide among 6 glasses.

Stir the gelatin into the Pimm's and slowly mix in the soda. Pour the mixture over the fruit in the glasses. Transfer the gelatins to the refrigerator and let chill and set for at least 4 hours.

Before serving, decorate the tops of the glasses with peach slices, strawberry halves, mint sprigs or borage flowers, and orange rind curls. To make orange rind curls, use a canelle knife to pare away the rind in strips, then wrap the strips tightly around a skewer or the handle of a wooden spoon. Slide them off after a minute or two.

Mango & passion fruit brûlées

PREPARATION TIME **10 MINUTES, PLUS CHILLING** • COOKING TIME **1–2 MINUTES**

131 CALORIES PER SERVING

SERVES **2**

- ½ small mango, peeled, pitted, and thinly sliced
- 1 passion fruit, halved and flesh scooped out
- ⅔ cup low-fat plain yogurt
- ½ cup crème fraîche or Greek yogurt
- ½ tablespoon confectioners' sugar
- a few drops of vanilla extract
- 1 tablespoon demerara or other raw sugar

Divide the mango slices between 2 ramekins.

Mix together the passion fruit flesh, yogurt, crème fraîche, confectioners' sugar, and vanilla extract in a bowl, then spoon the mixture over the mango. Tap each ramekin to level the surface.

Sprinkle with the demerara sugar, then cook the brûlées under a preheated hot broiler for 1–2 minutes, until the sugar has melted. Chill for about 30 minutes before serving.

Brûlée vanilla cheesecake

PREPARATION TIME **30 MINUTES, PLUS COOLING AND CHILLING** • COOKING TIME **30–35 MINUTES**

160 CALORIES PER SERVING

SERVES **6**

- 2½ cups nonfat cream cheese or ricotta cheese
- ⅓ cup granulated sweetener
- 1½ teaspoons vanilla extract
- finely grated rind of ½ orange
- 4 eggs, separated
- butter, for greasing
- 1 tablespoon confectioners' sugar, sifted
- 3 oranges, peeled and cut into segments

Mix together the cheese, sweetener, vanilla extract, orange rind, and egg yolks in a bowl until smooth.

In a large, clean bowl, beat the egg whites until softly peaking, then fold a large spoonful into the cheese mixture to loosen it. Add the remaining egg whites and gently fold them in.

Pour the mixture into a greased 8-inch springform cake pan and level the surface. Bake in a preheated oven, at 325°F, for 30–35 minutes, until well risen, golden brown, and just set in the center.

Turn off the oven and let the cheesecake stand inside the oven with the door slightly ajar to cool for 15 minutes. Remove from the oven, let cool, then chill in the refrigerator for 4 hours. (The cheesecake sinks slightly as it cools.)

Run a knife around the cheesecake, loosen the pan, and transfer to a serving plate. Dust the top with the sifted confectioners' sugar and caramelize the sugar with a chef's blowtorch. Serve within 30 minutes, while the sugar topping is still hard and brittle. Cut into 6 wedges and serve with the orange segments.

Passion fruit panna cotta

PREPARATION TIME **15 MINUTES, PLUS COOLING AND CHILLING** • COOKING TIME **5 MINUTES**

144 CALORIES PER SERVING

SERVES 2

- 1 gelatin sheet
- 4 passion fruit
- ½ cup reduced-fat crème fraîche or mascarpone cheese
- ¼ cup nonfat Greek yogurt
- ¼ cup water
- ½ teaspoon superfine or granulated sugar
- ½ vanilla bean, split lengthwise

Soften the gelatin sheet in cold water.

Halve the passion fruit and remove the seeds, working over a bowl to catch the juice. Reserve the seeds for decoration. Mix together the crème fraîche or mascarpone and yogurt with the passion fruit juice.

Put the measured water in a saucepan, add the sugar, and scrape in the vanilla beans seeds, then heat gently, stirring, until the sugar has dissolved. Drain the gelatin and add to the pan. Let cool.

Mix the gelatin mixture into the crème fraîche mixture, then pour into 2 ramekins or molds. Cover and chill for 6 hours or until set. Turn the panna cotta out of the molds onto serving plates by briefly immersing in hot water. Spoon over the reserved seeds and serve.

Strawberry roulade

PREPARATION TIME **30 MINUTES, PLUS COOLING** • COOKING TIME **8 MINUTES**

110 CALORIES PER SERVING

SERVES **8**

- vegetable oil, for greasing
- 3 eggs
- ⅔ cup granulated sugar
- 1 cup all-purpose flour, sifted
- 1 tablespoon hot water
- 3 cups hulled and quartered fresh or frozen strawberries, thawed if frozen
- 1 cup fromage blanc or plain yogurt
- confectioners' sugar, for dusting

Lightly grease a 13 x 9-inch jellyroll pan. Line with parchment paper to come about ½ inch above the sides of the pan. Lightly grease the paper.

Beat the eggs and sugar in a large bowl over a saucepan of hot water until pale and thick. Fold the flour into the egg mixture with the measured water. Pour the batter into the prepared pan and bake in a preheated oven, at 425°F, for 8 minutes, until golden and set.

Meanwhile, place a sheet of parchment paper 1 inch larger all around than the jellyroll pan on a clean, damp dish towel. Once cooked, immediately turn out the jellyroll face down onto the paper. Carefully peel off the lining paper. Roll the sponge up tightly with the new parchment paper inside. Wrap the dish towel around the outside and place on a wire rack until cool, then unroll carefully.

Add half the strawberries to the fromage blanc or yogurt and spread over the sponge. Roll the sponge up again and trim the ends. Dust with confectioners' sugar and decorate with a few strawberries.

Pure the remaining strawberries in a blender or food processor. Cut the roulade into 8 slices and serve with the strawberry sauce.

Plum & ricotta almond cake

PREPARATION TIME **30 MINUTES, PLUS COOLING AND CHILLING** • COOKING TIME **35–40 MINUTES**

150 CALORIES PER SERVING

SERVES 6

- butter, for greasing
- 8 sweet, ripe red plums, pitted and quartered
- 1 cup ricotta cheese
- ¼–⅓ cup granulated sweetener
- 3 eggs, separated
- ¼ teaspoon almond extract
- 4 teaspoons slivered almonds
- 2 tablespoons water
- 1 tablespoon confectioners' sugar, sifted

Grease an 8-inch springform cake pan and line the bottom with parchment paper. Arrange half the plums randomly over the cake pan.

Mix together the ricotta, ¼ cup of the sweetener, the egg yolks, and almond extract in a bowl until smooth. In a separate clean bowl, whisk the egg whites until stiff, moist peaks form. Fold into the ricotta mixture, then spoon it over the plums.

Sprinkle the top with the slivered almonds and bake in a preheated oven, at 325°F, for 30–35 minutes, until the cake is well risen, golden brown, and the center is just set. Check after 20 minutes and cover the top loosely with aluminum foil if the almonds seem to be browning too quickly.

Turn off the oven and let the cake cool for 15 minutes with the door slightly ajar. Remove from the oven, let cool, then chill well in the refrigerator.

Meanwhile, put the remaining plums and measured water in a saucepan, cover, and cook for 5 minutes until soft. Puree in a blender or food processor until smooth, mix in the remaining sweetener, if needed, then pour into a small pitcher.

To serve, remove the pan and lining paper and transfer the cake to a serving plate. Dust the top with the sifted confectioners' sugar and serve, cut into 6 wedges, with the sauce.

Calorie counter

	Average portion	Calories
FRUIT		
Apple, whole with core		
Cox's Pippin	4½ ounces (about 1 medium)	53
Golden Delicious	4½ ounces (about 1 medium)	50
Granny Smith	4½ ounces (about 1 medium)	52
Apple stewed with sugar	3¾ ounces (about 1 medium)	81
Apricots, flesh only	2¾ ounces (about 2 small)	25
Avocado, flesh only	5 ounces (about 1 cup cubed)	266
Banana	3½ ounces (about 1 small)	95
Blackberries	3½ ounces (about ⅔ cup)	25
Blueberries	1¾ ounces (about ⅓ cup)	35
Cherries, with pits	2¾ ounces (about ½ cup)	31
Clementine, unpeeled	2¾ ounces (about 1 small)	22
Figs	2 ounces (about 1 large)	24
Fruit Salad	5 ounces (about ⅔ cup)	77
Grapefruit, unpeeled	6 ounces (about ¾ medium)	20
Grapes	3½ ounces (about ⅔ cup)	60
Kiwi, with skin	2⅔ ounces (about 1 medium)	32
Lemon, unpeeled	2 ounces (about ½ medium)	8
Lime, unpeeled	1½ ounces (about ½ medium)	4
Melon, weighed with skin		
Cantaloupe	6⅓ ounces (about 1 cup)	23
Galia	7 ounces (about 1¼ cups)	30
Honeydew	7 ounces (about 1¼ cups)	38
Nectarine, with skin	5¼ ounces (about 1 large)	54
Orange, with skin	7 ounces (about 1 large)	52
Papaya, flesh only	5¼ ounces (about 1 cup diced)	50
Peach, with pit	5¼ ounces about (1 large)	45
Pear, whole with core	5¼ ounces (about 1 small)	54
Pineapple	2¾ ounces (about ½ cup diced)	33
Plum, with pit	2½ ounces (about 1 medium)	24
Raspberries	2 ounces (about ½ cup)	15
Satsuma/Madarin Orange, with skin		
	3 ounces (1 small)	23
Strawberries	3½ ounces (⅔ cup hulled and halved)	27
Watermelon, flesh only	7 ounces (1⅓ cups diced)	62
DRIED FRUIT, NUTS, AND SEEDS		
Almonds	½ ounce (about 2 tablespoons)	91
Apricots, dried	1 ounce (about 8 halves)	60
Brazil Nuts	⅓ ounce (about 2)	68
Cashew Nuts	⅓ ounce (about 1 tablespoon)	63
Cashew Nuts, roasted and salted		
	1 ounce (about 3½ tablespoons)	153
Chestnuts	1¾ ounces (about 4)	85
Cranberries, dried, sweetened		
	1 ounce (about 3 tablespoons)	82
Dates, dried, pitted	1¾ ounces (about 2 medium)	35
Figs, dried	¾ ounce (about 2 medium)	68
Hazelnuts	½ ounce (about 1 tablespoon)	65
Mixed Nuts	1½ ounces (about ⅓ cup)	243
Mixed Nuts and Raisins	1½ ounces (about ⅓ cup)	192
Peanuts, plain	½ ounce (about 1 tablespoon)	73
Peanuts, dry-roasted	1½ ounces (about ⅓ cup)	236
Pecans	¾ cup (about 3 tablespoons)	138
Pine Nuts	⅛ ounce (about ½ tablespoon)	34
Pistachio Nuts, roasted and salted		
	½ ounce (about 1 tablespoon)	60
Prunes, dried	2¼ ounces (about ½ cup)	93
Pumpkin Seeds	½ ounce (about 4 teaspoons)	91
Raisins, Golden	1 ounce (about 3 tablespoons	73
Raisins, seedless	1 ounce (about 3 tablespoons)	76
Sunflower Seeds	½ ounce (about 5 teaspoons)	96
Walnuts	¾ ounce (about 3 tablespoons)	138

	Average portion	Calories
VEGETABLES (RAW, PREPARED, UNLESS OTHERWISE STATED)		
Asparagus	4½ ounces (about 8 spears)	33
Beans		
Fava	4¼ ounces (about ¾ cup shelled)	58
Green	3 ounces (about ¾ cup pieces)	20
Runner	3 ounces (about ¾ cup pieces)	16
Beet	1½ ounces (about ½ medium)	18
Bell Pepper		
Green	5⅔ ounces (about 1 large)	24
Red	5⅔ ounces (about 1 large)	51
Yellow	5⅔ ounces (about 1 large)	42
Broccoli	3 ounces (about 1 cup florets)	20
Brussels Sprouts	3 ounces (about 5)	32
Cabbage		
Red	3 ounces (about 1 cup)	14
Savoy	3⅓ ounces (about 1 cup)	16
White	3⅓ ounces (about 1 cup)	13
Carrot	2 ounces (about 1 medium)	14
Cauliflower	3⅛ ounces (about 1 cup florets)	25
Celery	1 ounce (about 1 small stick)	2
Chile Pepper	⅛ ounce (about ¼ medium)	3
Corn Kernels	2 ounces (about ⅓ cup)	14
Corn on the Cob, weighed whole	7 ounces (1 ear)	123
Cucumber	1 ounce (about ¼ sliced)	2
Eggplant, broiled	3½ ounces (about ¼ small)	75
Fennel	3½ ounces (about 1 cup sliced)	11
Leek	2⅔ ounces (about 1 small)	16
Lettuce	2¾ ounces (about 1⅓ cups shredded)	13
Mushrooms	2¾ ounces (about 1 cup sliced)	10
Onion	5¼ ounces (about 1 large)	54
Parsnip	2¼ ounces (about ½ medium)	43
Peas	2½ ounces (about ½ cup)	55
Potatoes		
New, boiled	6 ounces (about 3 medium)	116
baked	6 ounces (about 1 large)	245
boiled	6 ounces (about 1 large)	126
mashed with butter	4¼ ounces (about 1 medium)	122
roasted	4½ ounces (about 1 medium)	151
Radishes	1¾ ounces (about ⅓ cup sliced)	6
Rutabaga	2 ounces (about ⅓ cup diced)	7
Scallions	⅛ ounce (about 2 small)	2
Spinach	3⅛ ounces (about 3 cups)	23
Squash, baked	2¼ ounces (about ½ cup)	21
Sweet Potato, baked	4½ ounces (about 1 small)	150
Tomato	3 ounces (about 1 small)	14
Tomato, broiled	3 ounces (about 1 small)	42
Tomatoes, Cherry	3⅛ ounces (about 5 medium)	16
Zucchini	3⅛ ounces (about 1 small)	17
CHEESE		
American, low-fat	1½ ounces	76
American, regular	1½ ounces	158
Brie	1½ ounces	144
Camembert	1½ ounces	116
Cheddar	1½ ounces	166
Cheese Spread	1 ounce	81
Cream Cheese, light	1 ounce	47
Cream Cheese, medium fat	1 ounce	74
Cottage, 4 percent fat	1½ ounces	36
Cottage, 2 percent fat	1½ ounces	28
Danish Blue	1 ounce	103
Dolcelatte	1½ ounces	158
Edam	1½ ounces	136
Emmental	1½ ounces	160

	Average portion	Calories
Feta	1¾ ounces	125
Gouda	1½ ounces	151
Monterey	1½ ounces	156
Mozzarella, fresh	2 ounces	141
Mozzarella, grated	2 ounces	164
Muenster	1½ ounces	155
Paneer	1½ ounces	130
Parmesan, freshly grated	¾ ounce	82
Ricotta	2 ounces	79
Roquefort	1 ounce	105
Stilton	1¼ ounces	143
EGGS		
Boiled	1¾ ounces (1 egg)	74
Fried	2 ounces (1 egg)	107
Poached	1¾ ounces (1 egg)	74
Omelet, Cheese	5¼ ounces (2 eggs)	399
Omelet, Plain	4¼ ounces (2 eggs)	180
Omelet, Spanish	5⅓ ounces (2 eggs)	229
Scrambled, no milk	3½ ounces (2 eggs)	160
Scrambled, with milk	4¼ ounces (2 eggs)	296
DAIRY		
Crème fraîche	1¾ ounces (about ¼ cup)	190
Crème fraîche, low fat	1¾ ounces (about ¼ cup)	85
Fromage blanc, plain	3½ ounces (about ⅓ cup)	113
Greek Yogurt, nonfat	3½ ounces (about ⅓ cup)	57
Milk		
Goat Milk	5 fluid ounces (about ⅓ cup)	88
Low-Fat Milk	5 fluid ounces (about ⅓ cup)	67
Skim Milk	5 fluid ounces (about ⅓ cup)	48
Soy Milk	5 fluid ounces (about ⅓ cup)	47
Whole Milk	5 fluid ounces (about ⅓ cup)	96
Sour Cream, Fat-Free	1 ounce (about 2 tablespoons)	29
Yogurt, plain nonfat	3½ ounces (about ⅓ cup)	46
MEAT		
Beef		
Braising Steak (braised)	5 ounces	315
Braising Steak (slow-cooked)	5 ounces	276
Ground, extra lean (stewed)	5 ounces	248
Tenderloin Steak (broiled)	5¾ ounces	316
Top Sirloin Steak (broiled)	5¾ ounces	287
Top Sirloin Steak strips (stir-fried)	3½ ounces	214
Tenderloin Steak (broiled)	5¾ ounces	292
Lamb		
Ground (stewed)	3⅛ ounces	187
Leg Cutlets (broiled)	3⅛ ounces	178
Loin Chops (broiled)	2½ ounces	149
Rack of Lamb (roasted)	3⅛ ounces	203
Shoulder Joint (roasted)	3⅛ ounces	212
Stewing (stewed)	4½ ounces	312
Organ Meats		
Liver, Lamb (fried)	3½ ounces	237
Liver, Ox (stewed)	2½ ounces	139
Liver, Pig (stewed)	2½ ounces	132
Livers, Chicken (fried)	2½ ounces	118
Pork, Bacon and Ham		
Bacon		
Collar Joint (boiled)	1⅔ ounces	88
Loin cutlets (broiled)	3½ ounces	191
Slices (dry-fried)	3½ ounces	295
Slices (broiled)	3½ ounces	214
Slices, dry-cured (broiled)	3½ ounces	257
Slices, smoked (broiled)	3½ ounces	293
Slices, sweet cure (broiled)	3½ ounces	258
Slices, Middle (broiled)	3½ ounces	307
Ground (stewed)	3⅛ ounces	172
Ham		
Ham, prosciutto	1⅔ ounces	105
Ham, premium	2 ounces	74
Pork Shoulder, cured	3½ ounces	103
Leg Joint (roasted)	3⅛ ounces	164
Loin Chops (broiled)	2⅔ ounces	140
Loin Cutlets (fried)	4¼ ounces	229
Loin Joint (pot-roasted)	3⅛ ounces	177
Pork, diced (stewed)	3⅛ ounces	166
Pork Cutlets (broiled)	4¾ ounces	228
Sparerib (broiled)	3¾ ounces	321
Sparerib (pot-roasted)	3⅛ ounces	181
Tenderloin of Pork (grilled)	4¼ ounces	240
POULTRY AND GAME		
Chicken		
Breast, skinless (broiled)	4½ ounces	192
Breast strips (stir-fried)	3⅛ ounces	145
Drumsticks, skinned (casseroled)	1⅔ ounces	87
Drumsticks, skinned (roasted)	1⅔ ounces	71
Leg Quarter (roasted)	5 ounces	345
Leg Quarter, skinned (casseroled)	5 ounces	257
Thighs, skinless, boneless (casseroled)	1⅔ ounces	81
Wings (broiled)	3½ ounces	274
Duck (roasted)	6½ ounces	361
Goose (roasted)	6½ ounces	590
Grouse (roasted)	5⅔ ounces	205
Pheasant (roasted)	5⅔ ounces	352
Pigeon (roasted)	4 ounces	215
Rabbit (stewed)	5⅔ ounces	182
Turkey		
Breast, skinless (broiled)	3⅛ ounces	140
Drumsticks, skinned (roasted)	3⅛ ounces	146
Mince (stewed)	3⅛ ounces	158
Strips (stir-fried)	3⅛ ounces	148
Thighs, diced skinless, boneless (casseroled)	3⅛ ounces	163
Venison (roasted)	4¼ ounces	198
FISH AND SEAFOOD		
Anchovies, in oil	⅓ ounce	28
Cod (baked)	4¼ ounces	115
Cod (poached)	4¼ ounces	113
Cod (steamed)	4¼ ounces	100
Cod, Smoked (poached)	4¼ ounces	121
Crab (boiled, dressed in shell)	4½ ounces	166
Crab, canned	1½ ounces	31
Flounder (broiled)	4½ ounces	125
Haddock (broiled)	4¼ ounces	125
Haddock (poached)	4¼ ounces	136
Haddock (steamed)	4¼ ounces	107
Haddock, Smoked (poached)	5⅓ ounces	201
Hake (broiled)	3½ ounces	113
Halibut (broiled)	5 ounces	175
Halibut (poached)	3¾ ounces	169
Halibut (steamed)	3¾ ounces	144

	Average portion (g)	Calories
Kipper (baked)	4½ ounces	267
Kipper (broiled)	4½ ounces	332
Lobster (boiled, dressed in shell)	8¾ ounces	258
Mackerel (broiled)	5 ounces	351
Monkfish (broiled)	2½ ounces	67
Mussels (boiled, shelled)	1½ ounces	42
Red Snapper	3 ounces	85
Salmon (broiled)	3 ounces	176
Salmon (steamed)	2¾ ounces	152
Salmon, Smoked	2 ounces	80
Sardines (broiled)	1½ ounces	78
Scallops (steamed, shelled)	2½ ounces	83
Shrimp (boiled, shelled)	2 ounces	59
Swordfish (broiled)	4½ ounces	174
Trout, Brown (steamed)	5½ ounces	209
Trout, Rainbow (steamed)	5½ ounces	209
Tuna, canned	1⅔ ounces	45
Tuna, raw	1⅔ ounces	61

RICE, PASTA, AND BEANS (UNCOOKED, UNLESS OTHERWISE STATED)

	Average portion (g)	Calories
Bulgur Wheat	3½ ounces (about ¾ cup)	338
Cannellini Beans, canned	3½ ounces (about ½ cup)	87
Chickpeas, canned	3½ ounces (about ½ cup)	115
Chickpeas, dried (boiled)	3½ ounces (about ⅔ cup)	121
Couscous	3½ ounces (about ½ cup)	364
Lentils, Green, canned	3½ ounces (about ½ cup)	118
Lentils, Green, dried (boiled)	3½ ounces (about ½ cup)	105
Lima Beans, canned	3½ ounces (about ⅓ cup)	77
Kidney Beans, canned	3½ ounces (about ⅓ cup)	100
Macaroni (boiled)	4½ ounces (about 1 cup)	108
Noodles, Egg (boiled)	4½ ounces (about ¾ cup)	78
Noodles (fried)	4½ ounces (about ¾ cup)	191
Rice		
Brown (boiled)	4½ ounces (about ⅔ cup)	176
White, glutinous (boiled)	4½ ounces (about ¾ cup)	82
White, regular (boiled)	4½ ounces (about ¾ cup)	154
Spaghetti (boiled)	4½ ounces (about 1 cup)	130
Spaghetti, whole-wheat (boiled)	4½ ounces (about 1 cup)	141

BREAD

	Average portion (g)	Calories
Ciabatta, plain	1¾ ounces (1 slice)	135
Croissants	2 ounces (1 medium)	224
French Bread	1½ ounces (1 small slice)	109
Garlic Bread	¾ ounce (1 small slice)	73
Hamburger/Hotdog Bun	1½ ounces (1 bun)	120
Hot Cross Buns	1¾ ounces (1 bun)	155
Italian Bread	1 ounce (1 large slice)	81
Muffins, English, white	2 ounces (1 muffin)	134
Pita Bread, white	2 ounces (6½-inch diameter)	165
Rolls		
White, crusty	1¾ ounces (1 large roll)	131
White, soft	1⅔ ounces (2 dinner rolls)	114
Whole-Wheat	1⅔ ounces (2 dinner rolls)	117
Sliced		
Multigrain	1¼ ounces (about 1¼ slices)	92
Rye	1 ounce (about 1 slice)	83
White	1½ ounces (about 1½ slices)	94
Whole-Wheat	1½ ounces (about 1½ slices)	93
Soda Bread, Irish	4½ ounces (one thick slice)	267
Tortilla, soft	1¾ ounces (one 8-inch)	146

CEREALS

	Average portion (g)	Calories
Bran Flakes	1 ounce (about ¾ cup)	95
Cheerios	1 ounce (about 1 cup)	103
Corn Flakes	1 ounce (about 1 cup)	108
Frosted Flakes	1 ounce (about ¾ cup)	113
Muesli	1¾ ounces (about ⅔ cup)	184
Oat Flakes	1 ounce (about ¾ cup)	107
Oatmeal, with milk and water	5⅔ ounces (about ⅔ cup)	133
Oatmeal, with water	5⅔ ounces (about ⅔ cup)	78
Oatmeal, with whole milk	5⅔ ounces (about ⅔ cup)	186
Puffed Wheat	¾ ounce (about 1⅓ cups)	64
Raisin Bran	2 ounces (about 1 cup)	187
Rice Pops	1 ounce (about 1 cup)	111
Wheat, Shredded	1⅔ ounces (1 biscuit)	150
Wheat, Shredded, mini	1⅔ ounces (about 1 cup)	154
Whole-Wheat Biscuits	1⅓ ounces (about 2 biscuits)	134

PRESERVES AND SPREADS

	Average portion (g)	Calories
Honey	½ ounce (about 1 tablespoon)	91
Preserves	½ ounce (about 2 teaspoons)	39
Lemon Curd	½ ounce (1 tablespoon)	42
Marmalade	½ ounce (about 2 teaspoons)	26
Peanut Butter, chunky	¾ ounce (about 1 tablespoon)	152
Peanut Butter, smooth	¾ ounce (about 1 tablespoon)	156
Yeast Extract	⅛ ounce (about 1 teaspoon)	9

DIPS

	Average portion (g)	Calories
Guacamole	1⅔ ounces (about 3 tablespoons)	58
Hummus	1 ounce (about 2 tablespoons)	56
Tzatziki	1½ ounces (about 3 tablespoons)	30

COLD DRINKS AND JUICES

	Average portion (g)	Calories
Apple Juice	5⅔ fluid ounces (about ⅔ cup)	61
Carrot Juice	5⅔ fluid ounces (about ⅔ cup)	38
Cola	5⅔ fluid ounces (about ⅔ cup)	66
Cola, diet	5⅔ fluid ounces (about ⅔ cup)	Trace
Grapefruit Juice	5⅔ fluid ounces (about ⅔ cup)	53
Lemon-Flavored Soda	5⅔ fluid ounces (about ⅔ cup)	35
Lemon-Flavor Soda, diet	5⅔ fluid ounces (about ⅔ cup)	Trace
Orange Juice, fresh	5⅔ fluid ounces (about ⅔ cup)	53
Pineapple Juice	5⅔ fluid ounces (about ⅔ cup)	66
Pomegranate Juice	5⅔ fluid ounces (about ⅔ cup)	70

HOT DRINKS

	Average portion (g)	Calories
Cappuccino, with low-fat milk	6¾ fluid ounces (about ¾ cup)	46
Coffee, with low-fat milk	6¾ fluid ounces (about ¾ cup)	13
Coffee, with skim milk	6¾ fluid ounces (about ¾ cup)	8
Coffee, with whole milk	6¾ fluid ounces (about ¾ cup)	15
Hot Chocolate, with low-fat milk	6¾ fluid ounces (about ¾ cup)	135
Hot Chocolate, with skimd milk	6¾ fluid ounces (about ¾ cup)	112
Hot Chocolate, with whole milk	6¾ fluid ounces (about ¾ cup)	171
Latte, with low-fat milk	6¾ fluid ounces (about ¾ cup)	60
Latte, with skimd milk	6¾ fluid ounces (about ¾ cup)	33
Latte, with whole milk	6¾ fluid ounces (about ¾ cup)	85
Tea, black	6¾ fluid ounces (about ¾ cup)	Trace
Tea, Chinese	6¾ fluid ounces (about ¾ cup)	2
Tea, green	6¾ fluid ounces (about ¾ cup)	Trace
Tea, herbal	6¾ fluid ounces (about ¾ cup)	2
Tea, with low-fat milk	6¾ fluid ounces (about ¾ cup)	13
Tea, with skim milk	6¾ fluid ounces (about ¾ cup)	8
Tea, with whole milk	6¾ fluid ounces (about ¾ cup)	15

Index

Acknowledgments

PICTURE ACKNOWLEDGMENTS

Getty Images/Blend Images/John Fedele 22; Mike Harrington 27; Photo by Ira Heuvelman-Dobrolyubova 18; Andersen Ross 17; J. Shepherd 19.

Octopus Publishing Group/Stephen Conroy 93, 94, 111, 131; Will Heap 4; Lis Parsons 1 right, 38, 41, 43, 45, 48, 49, 55, 56, 60, 68, 74, 80, 83, 89, 99, 103, 116, 122, 135, 137; Bill Reavell 121; Russell Sadur 20, 28; Gareth Sambidge 59, 126; William Shaw 46, 71, 77, 104; Simon Smith 1 left, 51, 54, 66, 69, 96, 113.

Thinkstock/Bananastock 29; George Doyle 11, 23; iStockphoto 9, 15, 21; Stockbyte 32; Wavebreak Media 7, 25, 31.

Publisher: Sarah Ford
Managing Editor: Clare Churly
Designer: Eoghan O'Brien
Layouts by Jeremy Tiltson
Picture Library Manager: Jennifer Veall
Senior Production Manager: Peter Hunt